RECONNECTING
the GENERATIONS

Empowering God's people, young and old,
to live, worship and serve together

Daphne Kirk

First published in 2001 by
KEVIN MAYHEW LTD
Buxhall
Stowmarket
Suffolk IP14 3BW

9 8 7 6 5 4 3 2 1 0

ISBN 1 84003 834 9
Catalogue No 1500464

Cover design by Angela Self
Edited by Jonathan Bugden and Elisabeth Bates
Typeset by Elisabeth Bates
Printed and bound in Great Britain

Contents

Introduction 5

God's vision for the generations 7

The interdependence of the generations 15

Every generation is crucial,
    every generation is strategic 27

Prophetic words for the generations today 31

Empowering a generation: the young people 39

Rescuing a generation: the children 43

Discipling the youngest generation 53

Bridging the gap 65

Discovering and keeping 73

Passing it on! 85

From hiddenness to holiness 93

Generational anointing 107

The generations together 115

Taking the nations 125

Prayer 127

My thanks to Bill Beckham who travels the nations inspiring many like myself. He encouraged me to write this book, and has given wisdom when I have so needed it.

Also to my friend Matthew E. Scheff. We have cheered each other on building bridges across the generations, but thanks most of all for being a friend. Take the nations, Matt!

Introduction

This is a wake-up call, bringing awareness that will effect change in our own lives, and the lives of those coming after us . . . the young people and children who announce the arrival of the next generation! We are all responsible for the next generation. We can change their destiny, and we can be the springboards that send them into their future with a fire and passion for Jesus to fulfil the great commission as they take the Gospel into the darkest places on earth.

We live in the context of generations that have come before and those which will follow. It is easy to go through life unaware of the significance of the context into which we were born and how it affects us from day to day. There is a growing interest in the topic of the generations, the search for personal genealogies and identities, and a growing concern about the legacy that we will leave future generations.

Many are aware of negative spiritual influences from the past still affecting their lives, and by breaking free of these influences bring change to their own lives and the lives of their children. However as a Ugandan pastor put it, 'Daphne, you have just hit a missing link. We break curses over Christians and non-Christians alike in our country, but we always feel that there is something missing. I have just discovered what. We don't know how to live in the blessing.' The blessing that comes from the heart of God who wants to open a river of blessing that will flow 'even to a thousand generations' (Exodus 20).

He wants us to partner with him in releasing the good from generations past and changing the destiny of the generations to come . . . the children, their children and their children's children!

When considering the generations we can look at them from different perspectives:

1. Our individual generational lines: the children we have had, our children's children, and our past heritage.

2. The generations corporately: our identity and responsibility in the broader sense. A whole generation having corporate identity and responsibility.

3. Our spiritual generations: those with whom we identify because of spiritual relationship. Mothers, fathers, daughters, sons, etc.

The word 'children' can apply both to our own children (of any age) by physical birth, and to 'spiritual children'.

In this book we will be looking at all these aspects; many times they are inter-linked and the thrust of the book can mostly be applied to one or all of these, leaving the reader to make the application as they choose. However, at certain times specific application is made.

Reconnecting the Generations is about changing the way we see things, about changing our values. It is not about structures.

God's vision for the generations

Have you ever given thought to the fact that the generations are foundationally significant in the plans of God? That they were, and still are an orchestration of the Almighty God? Isaiah 41:4: says, 'Who has performed and done this? Calling and guiding the destiny of the generations from the beginning, I, the Lord, am with the first and with the last – I am he' (Amplified Bible).

The generations weren't a mistake. Nothing God does is an accident. God spoke and he said, 'Stars be!' and the stars were and, behold, they were very good. He said 'Mountains be!' and the mountains were, and behold, they were very good. In the same way he looked and he said, 'Generations be!' and said, 'Behold, they are very good'. The generations were perfectly part of God's creative plan.

When he breathed life into Adam in Genesis Chapter 2, he sent his own life-flow straight from his heart and the generations began.

God is timeless, yet in these verses he sets himself within human time locating himself at the beginning and at the end of the generations, 'with the first and with the last'.

In Revelation 22:13, from the throne of heaven, he reminds us, 'I am Alpha and Omega, the beginning and the end.' The eternal, timeless God, setting himself within the parameters of our mortal time as the beginning and the end . . . of the generations. They were breathed into being from the breath of God and one day will return to him as he welcomes them into the very throne room of heaven.

Meanwhile he has made a commitment that he is 'calling and guiding the destiny of the generations'. He has a perfect plan for them, and until the day they return to him has promised to watch over and guide them into their destiny. 'He will endure as long as the sun, as long as the moon, through all generations' (Psalm 72:5). He will be there for them, not one generation is outside his care.

God has given us comparatively few pages of his Word. This is the book that many have died for; this is the written expression of himself. Why then would he use precious space with pages of genealogies, if they were not of supreme importance? It is precisely because they are of such importance in his purposes and plans that he spreads them out before us.

It is not without significance that the Old Testament closes with the promise of the spirit of Elijah (Malachi 4) bringing healing between the generations, and the New Testament begins with a genealogy. The genealogy of Jesus! From the beginning God had been 'guiding and calling forth' this generational line for the birth of his Son, each little baby taking their place until God's own Son was born in a manger. He chose to come into that generational flow until, in his death, he became the end of that particular line of the generations, the line of David.

This baby, the Lamb of God, the 'beginning and the end', entered the generations so that his salvation would flow and his throne be established on this earth.

Just as the generations brought forth Jesus, in the perfect timing of God, so each person is brought forth within their generation for 'such a time as this' (Esther 4:14). You are important, the generations before you, around you and those that are yet to come are important, and the exciting thing that you will discover is that you can influence the present and the future and inherit from the past!

Why did God create the generations?

His throne is from generation to generation

'Oh, Lord, you remain for ever. Your throne from generation to generation.' God is building a throne from generation to generation, where he can be seated, and seen to be Lord of all. (Lamentations 5:19)

He didn't just establish his throne with one generation; every generation is called to be a continuation of the throne of God on this earth.

His salvation and mercy are from generation to generation

My righteousness will be for ever. My salvation from generation to generation. (Isaiah 51:8)

Salvation is about God's covenant applied to generation after generation. Each generation is responsible for passing on the good news of redemption to their generation and the generations coming after them so that his salvation is established on earth.

His dominion is from generation to generation

How great are his signs, how mighty his wonders. His kingdom is an eternal kingdom: his dominion endures from generation to generation. (Daniel 4:3)

Dominion means 'territory with one ruler', the generations are God's territory with him as the appointed ruler over them.

The plans of his heart are to all generations

'The counsel of the Lord stands for ever. The plans of his heart to all generations.' The generations were created by God to be the vehicle for him to reveal and manifest plans that were born in his heart. (Psalm 33:11)

Each generation has a responsibility to know his heart and live out his plans so that the next generation can continue in them and so bring every generation to the climax of history at the throne of God.

His renown (the fame of his name) endures through all generations

But you, O Lord, sit enthroned for ever; your renown [the fame of your name] endures through all generations. (Psalm 102:12)

This is my name for ever, the name by which I am to be remembered from generation to generation [I AM]. (Exodus 3:15)

The God of Abraham, Isaac and Jacob – three generations – (Exodus 3:15) is known in every generation.

Generations may pass but his fame is known throughout history, his name is the name that has been and will be on the lips of every generation.

His faithfulness is from generation to generation

Your faithfulness continues through all generations. (Psalm 119:90)

As one generation passes and another comes, the never ending, never failing faithfulness of God continues towards them. They all bear the indelible marks of his faithfulness.

God has big plans for the generations.

Exodus 20 talks about the curse being to the third and fourth generation but showing mercy to a thousand. It is the heart of God for there to be a thousand generations of blessing, but when we cry out for that blessing to flow, we so often present God with fractured generations for it to flow through.

At weddings we say, 'What God has joined together, let no

one put asunder.' He joined us together generationally and yet in so many ways we put asunder, by the words of our mouths, the attitude of our hearts and the way we relate to each other.

Jesus prayed in John 17, 'that they would be one'. Across the streams and denominations, between the races and the genders, barriers are being broken down. We can begin to see the prayer of Jesus being answered. However, there is one area that most people haven't noticed. It is that, generationally, we are not one.

We can rest assured that if Jesus prayed, then generational unity is possible and will happen.

I had been watching someone on television with a great healing ministry and said, 'Oh God, I wish you had given me a healing ministry like his.' He quietly replied, 'Daphne, I have given you a healing ministry. I have called you to be an instrument of healing to my broken, fractured body.'

Suddenly, I felt so humble, 'Oh Lord, that I have the privilege of being a part of the healing of your precious body, where generationally we are fractured.' Today God is bringing that healing to his body and this book is about understanding God's heart towards the generations and how significant they are to him.

Everything God does, he does for a purpose, and the generations are part of his perfect plan. Understanding this will help us to walk in the generational blessing instead of living in the shadow of the curse. It is about holiness and preparation of the bride.

Generational authority and impact

The people of Israel understood the impact they could have on the generations after them, and the authority they had been given to speak into them.

We read in Esther 9:25-32:

But, when Esther brought the matter before the King, he commanded in writing that Haman's wicked scheme, which he had devised against the Jews, should return on his own head and that he and his son should be hanged on the gallows. And, therefore, they called these days 'Purim' after the word 'Pur', meaning lot (verses 25-26).

And the Jews ordained (verse 27) and took upon themselves and their descendants and all who joined them that, without fail, every year, they would keep these two days at the appointed time as it was written.

And that these days should be remembered, imprinted on their minds, and kept throughout every generation, in every family, in every province, and every city . . . as they ordained for themselves and their descendants in the matter of their fasts. (Esther 9:28, 31)

If a godly man or woman of authority stood up today and said, 'I am ordaining that, from this generation onwards, this matter will be', we would wonder how anyone could make a declaration over generations that were as yet unborn. Esther knew, and the Jewish people knew, that this was possible because of their lifestyle and faith.

God wants to restore that authority to us so we can start commanding and decreeing to the generations as yet unborn and so that people will once again understand how to perpetuate authority from generation to generation.

Another person who understood generational impact was Mary who said, 'All generations shall call me blessed. His mercy is on those that fear him from generation to generation.' (Luke 1:48)

She knew she was carrying the Son of the Almighty God, and that this moment would have an impact on the generations to come. Her immediate reaction was one of generational impact.

We too are commissioned by God to be vehicles of change and impact on the generations to come.

Psalm 145:4: 'One generation shall praise your works to another.'

This is how the Jewish people today still keep Purim. One generation remembers with the next generation, the father tells the son and he tells his children. As generational communication and relationship is restored we will again be able to decree to the generations to come and speak godly authority into them.

When God does something for us and we have a story to tell, most of the time we tell it. 'One generation shall praise your works to another.'

We are all called to be an example and communicate generationally. Children and young people have a responsibility generationally too. This isn't just about any one particular age. We are all a part of the restoration that is needed.

The interdependence of the generations

As our hearts begin to burn with God's vision for the generations, so we will begin to have his passion for their restoration, and a vision of their wholeness.

The generations were intended to be interdependent; it was never the heart of God that they should become insular and self-sufficient. They were created to flow together in complete unity to bring glory to his name.

'By this shall all men know that you are my disciples when you have love one for another' (John 13:35). And this included love between the generations.

If we lose sight of this interdependence usually one of two things happens in our attitudes. Either one generation will have a very benevolent attitude to the other or a generation will retreat into insularity not realising that they too are losing out.

> But now God has set members, each one of them, in the body just as he pleased. (1 Corinthians 12:18)

God has set each generation, *each one* – the children, the young people, the middle-aged, the elderly, the married, the single – *just as he pleased,* 'calling them forth from the beginning' (Isaiah 41:4).

> And, if they were all one member, where would the body be? But now, indeed, there are many members, yet one body. And the eye cannot say to the hand, 'I have no need of you' nor again the head to the feet, 'I have no need of you'. No, much rather those members of the

body which seem to be weaker are necessary.
(1 Corinthians 12)

If this Scripture is read with the generations in mind, the honest response is that most of the time we say by our actions that we have no need of the generations around us.

'I don't need you in my prayer life', 'I don't need you when I'm winning the lost', 'I don't need you when I need a friend', *but* 'Can the hand say to the foot I have no need of you? No, much rather those members of the body which seem weaker are necessary.'

Which generation to you seems weaker? Some might say the children, others the elderly, or the teenagers. The teenagers might call the adults the weaker members. If you are honest there is probably a generation of whom you would say, 'Well, they're the weaker ones'.

God says, 'much rather those members (that generation) of the body which seem to be weaker are necessary'. Whatever generation you think is weaker, is very necessary to the rest of us.

I am not advocating that we have to do everything together. Families don't do everything together all the time. That would only be true of a dysfunctional family. Children do things by themselves and so do the teenagers, parents have times together, but each member is needed, loved and wanted by the others. Nothing will tear a functional family apart because they are bound together with love.

Generally in the body of Christ, we've got it round the other way. We need, love and want our peers, and, sometimes, as a special arrangement, we will be with the other generations. God wants to turn this around so that although we may do things separately, if anyone spoke against, or tried to divide our hearts from the other generations, we would instinctively feel the wounding of the body and be an instrument of healing.

From that bonding in spirit, we will begin to love the generations around us, seeing them as part of God's plan. Let's examine relationships in Scripture that were powerful and life changing across the generations:

Timothy and Paul

Paul wrote to Timothy, 'I have been reminded of your sincere faith which first lived in your grandmother Lois, and in your mother Eunice and, am persuaded now lives in you also' (2 Timothy 1:5).

Paul saw the heritage in the life of Timothy. His faith was nurtured by two proceeding generations, which gave him a foundation on which Paul was able to build.

I have noticed solidity that is quite unique in people who have a heritage like Timothy. Where parents and grandparents spiritually nurture their children they lay foundations in those children's lives that will remain. This legacy is the godly right of every child. They need spiritual nurturing from the older generations in the same way that they need nurturing in the other areas of their lives.

Timothy was able to relate to an older man and receive wisdom and counsel from him because he already knew the value of listening to and serving those older than himself. Paul saw the fruit in Timothy's life.

However, Timothy was also a blessing to Paul as he helped with the ministry God had given him and was able to continue Paul's vision. As Paul got older he was dependent on Timothy to further the work that he had begun and to remain his most loyal friend. Just as Timothy had needed Paul, so Paul needed Timothy.

If we neglect to pass on to the next generation, all that we have will die with us, our visions, our anointing, and our dreams.

Ruth and Naomi

> Ruth said, '[Naomi] your people will be my people and your God my God.' (Ruth 1:16)

This loyalty may have been because Naomi had passed on to her the wonderful works of God, and the stories of her homeland, so by passing on her heritage to Ruth it had caught her heart. Perhaps she showed Ruth that there was a relationship she could have that was stronger than any national ties. Whatever the reason, such was the strength of the relationship that the younger woman was prepared to go with the older.

That is what God is looking for. A lasting impact on the next generation, creating in them such a desire that they say, 'Where you go, I go: and your God will be my God.'

When Ruth and Naomi returned together to Bethlehem it was Naomi who guided her through the customs and traditions of the culture in which she had chosen to live. Finally the day came, after Ruth had married Boaz that she gave birth to Obed (the father of Jesse, the father of David) and the women said to Naomi:

> 'Praise be to the Lord, who this day has not left you without a kinsman-redeemer. He will renew your life and sustain you in your old age. For your daughter-in-law, who loves you and who is better to you than seven sons, has given him birth.' Then Naomi took the child, laid him in her lap and cared for him. (Ruth 4:14-16)

Naomi was also the recipient in their relationship. The older woman, caring for the younger, the younger caring for the older. Generationally bonded in love with each other, just as Paul would later exhort Titus:

> 'Teach the older women to be reverent in the way they live, not to be slanderers or addicted to much wine, but to teach what is good. Then they can train the younger

women to love their husbands and children, to be self-controlled and pure, to be busy, to be kind, and to be subject to their husbands, so that no one will malign the word of God.' (Titus 2:3-5)

The responsibility given to the older women is quite clear here. This support was a natural outcome when generations lived with or near each other. In today's fractured society younger women are bereft of that support and security during the vulnerable years of marriage, careers, new homes, parenthood and developing relationships. Here is a command to Titus to teach the older women to pick up that responsibility.

Where younger women go astray, the older women need to examine themselves and repent of the lack of input into their lives. One generation was created to love, support and nurture the other.

I love having younger women in my life – they are my friends! Discipleship generationally is so natural.

Ruth and Naomi's relationship can also be a picture of when somebody is born again into the Kingdom of God. We need to be there and say to people, 'If you will come with me to this other land called the Kingdom of God, I'll be there for you.' So they will respond saying, 'Where you go, I will go. Your people will be my people. Your God will be my God.'

When older generations impact the younger they create faith and vision, and become their heroes. Let's cry out to God and start to make a difference. What a mobilisation could take place if every generation rose up and took its place and impacted the others.

David and Solomon

Now Lord, God of Israel, keep for your servant David, my father, the promises you made to him when you said,

'You shall never fail to have a man to sit before me on the throne of Israel, if only your sons are careful in all they do to walk before me as you have done.' (1 Kings 8:25)

God said to David, 'If your sons copy you, you will always have a king on the throne.' That is called modelling, or learning by watching, and then copying. God saw the power of the life of David, and he knew that the throne of David would be secured if his sons kept their eyes on the relationship their father had with his God. Solomon had a role model.

This generational modelling can take place quite naturally within the family. How often have you said, 'I'm just like my mum' or 'My dad used to do that'? Your mum and dad didn't sit down and say, 'Now you become like me.' You just picked it up. That's how God wants it to be in a very positive way.

He wants us to be role models for each other but more than that I believe God is looking for relationships where the Holy Spirit can say to others, 'Be careful in all you do to walk before me as this person has done.' Such a relationship can be called mentoring, discipleship or fathering. One generation, whether physical or spiritual, showing the other the way.

God is looking for a generation which is worthy of watching, and which will secure the testimony of Jesus on the earth for the generation to come; and a generation, which will respect their fathers, seeking counsel and wisdom as they follow in their footsteps.

Samuel and Eli

The story of Samuel and Eli as told in 1 Samuel chapters 1 and 2 shows how powerful are two generations living and serving God together, and how they need each other:

Eli was an instrument of peace to Hannah as she cried out for the birth of a child. Later, when she bought Samuel to Eli he gave him a home, even though his own children had left home and were not a good testimony to his fathering! Samuel then served Eli in the temple and was a blessing to him. It's worth noting that, without Eli, Samuel did not recognise the voice of God, yet without Samuel, Eli might not have heard the message from God.

I have heard older people say, 'My children have grown up and they've left home. I have done my bit.' We need more people with the heart of Eli. Eli cared for Samuel but they needed each other, it was redemptive for both of them. Even though he had made mistakes with his own sons he was prepared to 'have another go'! Some of the greatest learning experiences we have are in the mistakes we made.

There is nothing in the Word of God that absolves us from responsibility to the children. We are all custodians of the generations; the children belong to all of us.

When God asks us to take an interest in a child he trusts us with his most precious possession, and so do the parents. God is going to bring children to us who have no spiritual parents at all. How are they going to know what a godly family is like? How are they going to know what a godly heritage is if we are all so cocooned that we are not prepared to take them to our hearts?

God is raising up a generation who will make themselves available for a generation of children.

The cry is already going out in society. The Prince of Wales was quoted in the press as wanting millions of retired people to volunteer as surrogate parents to break the inner-city cycle of depravation and crime. He sees the biggest problem for vulnerable young people as being that they have no caring adults to turn to for support. Is it possible to galvanise millions of retired people across the country to take up the call?

What a challenge for the body of Christ, to mobilise an army from one generation to rescue another. We need each other!

A little child and the adults

Jesus showed how a generation of children can show the previous generations the way.

> Unless you change and become like little children you will never enter the kingdom of heaven.(Matthew 18:3)

How often have you longed to be great in the kingdom? Jesus said that the children would show us the way. They, by their simple uncomplicated love and faith are our role models.

As we release children to be all that they are called to be in the kingdom so we release the modelling we need. Sadly I see men and women desiring to be great in the kingdom but having no contact with the younger generation. They have lost their role models!

The following is a true story. A group was meeting and as one of the members was absent because she had a migraine headache, the leader asked one of the children to pray for her. 'Dear Lord Jesus,' prayed the child 'please take away her headache, take away the pain and don't let her die.' Everybody laughed and began to explain to the child that one did not die from a migraine headache!

The next day the leader telephoned to enquire how the migraine headache was. 'Haven't you heard?' came the reply, 'It wasn't a migraine, it was meningitis.' And she did not die!

A simple spirit response so easily eludes us as we get older. We need each other!

When ministering, I took a young child with me. When he arrived home his mother asked if he had prayed. 'Oh yes,' he said, 'but not like those adults. I just pray quick prayers and God hears me.' That is the sort of prayer warrior I will take with me anywhere; he has the confidence to know God hears him and answers. Each generation taking vision from the others, each generation being vision to the others.

Matthew 21 tells how Jesus came riding into Jerusalem,

and everybody from the youngest to the eldest was shouting, 'Hosanna, blessed is he who comes in the name of the Lord.' Then Jesus went into the temple, healed a blind man, and knocked the tables over. As Jesus knocked over yet another table, the children were shouting, 'Hosanna, blessed is he who comes in the name of the Lord.' Crash! Bang! 'Blessed is he who comes in the name of the Lord.' The children were still shouting while it seems that the adults had all disappeared. Then the Pharisees and Sadducees said to Jesus, 'Tell those children to be quiet!'

And Jesus said, 'Out of the mouths of children and infants you have provided perfect praise' (Matthew 21:16; Amplified).

Here were the children showing the adults how to praise Jesus unconditionally, and wholeheartedly. We need them as much as they need us.

Psalm 68:6: 'He places the solitary in families.'

God wants people who are alone restored to their natural environment, to be included and be part of family.

Family is an intergenerational environment where God intended we would all feel loved, accepted and secure.

Often I see that if a husband goes away – and almost definitely if a wife goes away – the one left at home gets invited out to meals and gets loved because they are alone. But there are single people who come home every night with nobody to cook a meal for him or her. Nobody says to them, 'How can I care for you?'

Children love single people. We need to welcome those who live alone and restore the community of family to them. When the single are younger they still have the heart cry for family, when they are older their heritage can be our blessing as the following shows:

Until late this century we spent time with people of all generations. Now many baby boomers may not have much contact with old folk until they are relatively old themselves. That is because we group people by age. We put our 3-year-olds in day care centres, our 13-year-olds in sports activities and our 80-year-olds in senior citizens' homes. We segregate the old for many reasons, prejudice, ignorance, lack of good alternatives. There are problems with the age segregation. Ten-year-olds grouped together will form a *Lord of the Flies* culture. A group of people aged 2 to 80 will fall into a natural age hierarchy that nurtures and teaches them all. My life is richer because of the time I spent with my elders . . . I have a better understanding of our history. To learn from the old we must love them – not in the abstract but in the flesh. We must work together to build the kinds of cities that allow us to care for one another.

Restore the shout from generation to generation

One generation shall praise your works to another. (Psalm 145:4)

Let's restore the shout of praise, the testimony of God's greatness as a flow between the generations, each generation passing on to the other! It will maintain the dominion of God on the earth; it will establish his throne and heal his wounded body.

Very silently the enemy has fractured the generations, without much of the Body of Christ noticing. Now is the time to wake up, to activate healing and be restored. One generation exalting the name of the Lord to another.

This interactive flow causes each generation to rise up and see the fulfilment of Acts 2:17, 18, 21:

In these last days I will pour out my Spirit on all people [men, women and children]. Your sons and daughters will prophesy, your young men will see visions, your old men dream dreams. Even on my servants, both men and women, I will pour out my Spirit in those days, and they will prophesy . . . everyone [men, women and children] who calls on the name of the Lord will be saved.

One generation, by their walk of love and obedience can secure the destiny of another.

These are the commands, decrees and laws the Lord your God directed me to teach you to observe in the land that you are crossing the Jordan to possess, so that you, your children and their children after them may fear the Lord your God as long as you live. (Deuteronomy 6:1-2a)

Take hold of the future, it is not outside our influence; we prepare the way for them. I heard how the father of Venus and Serena Williams, the 'all-conquering tennis champions', wrote down everything his as yet unborn daughters would need to succeed. In difficult times the girls refer back to these documents. He says, 'That's why they can't break this family down. Because everything was written before they came out of their mother's womb.'

The future of Venus and Serena was laid out before their birth by a father with a passion. We have a Father with a passion for his children as yet unborn. Their future has already been written down by their Father and if we will own the vision we will be able to say, 'Everything our unborn need to succeed is written down in the Word, and in our lives. That is why they can't break us apart. Because everything was written before they came out of their mother's womb.'

They are dependent on us, to 'fully obey the Lord [our] God and carefully follow all his commands' so the fruit of our womb will be blessed.

Every generation is crucial, every generation is strategic*

To the Lord your God belong the highest heavens, the earth and everything in it. Yet the Lord set his affection on your forefathers and loved them, and he chose you, their descendants above all nations. (Deuteronomy 10:15)

God has chosen each generation; he has set his love on each one. The generations do not roll on and on with no sense of destiny or purpose. They are guided by Almighty God (Isaiah 41:4) who desires that the destiny of each individual and the generation as a whole be fulfilled.

The characteristics of a righteous generation

How can we identify a generation which truly knows its God?

He who has clean hands and a pure heart, who does not lift up his soul to an idol or swear by what is false, he will receive blessing from the Lord and vindication from God his Saviour. Such is the generation of those who seek him, who seek your face, O God of Jacob. (Psalm 24:4-6)

Blessed is the man who fears the Lord, who finds great delight in his commands. His children will be mighty in the land; the generation of the upright will be blessed. (Psalm 112:1-2)

* Billy Graham

A righteous generation will be totally happy living in purity of word and deed, while keeping their eyes on Jesus. That generation will be seen to be blessed; they will be totally vindicated by the hand of the Lord. The generation after them will be mighty in the land that has become their inheritance. What a vision to keep before us! 'A royal priesthood, a chosen generation.'

Inheritance withheld, inheritance given

Each generation has the opportunity of entering into their destiny, and by so doing secures the destiny of the next generation. God has purposes for each generation, 'to give them a hope and a future'. However, each generation has the choice of receiving their inheritance or of passing it by:

> Not a man of this evil generation shall see the good land I swore to give your forefathers. (Deuteronomy 1:35)

> And the little ones that you have said would be taken captive, your children who do not know good from bad – they will enter the land. I will give it to them and they will take possession of it. (Deuteronomy 1:39)

The Israelites, through their disobedience, lost the inheritance for their day, they never entered the land, and the generation following received the blessing. God did not intend them to wander aimlessly in the desert, he loved them enough to deliver them out of the hands of Pharaoh and he loved them enough to settle them in their promised land.

Each generation has a destiny, each generation must choose to walk in it, or pass it by. God will fulfil his purpose and plans, and is looking for a generation who will be all that he has called them to be in their season on this earth.

We are born for a certain generation

> When David had served God's purpose in his generation, he fell asleep. (Acts 13:36)

We are all born to fulfil a purpose, not just at any time in history but perfectly placed in our own generation. We are not born a generation too early, or a generation too late.

So significant are we to God that he not only chose us before the foundation of the world (Ephesians 1:4) but he chose the very moment in history that we were to be born into. We each have a purpose to fulfil the destiny of our lives within the destiny of our generation, just as was spoken of Noah: 'Noah was just and perfect in his generations and Noah served God' (Genesis 6:8-9).

Specific revelation for a specific generation

God has specific revelation for a specific generation. God is beyond time but he speaks according to the generations. We see this clearly in the scientific world as one generation's acquired knowledge is passed on to another. God is unfolding his plans and purposes from generation to generation.

> You will be able to understand my insight into the mystery of Christ, which was not made known to men in other generations as it has now been revealed by the Spirit to God's holy apostles and prophets. (Ephesians 3:4-5)

> It was not with our fathers that the Lord made this covenant but with us, with all of us who are alive here today. (Deuteronomy 5:3)

Previous generations prepared the way for the time when God would reveal new truths for the next. God has finely orchestrated the unfolding of his revelation generation upon generation until he reaches his explosive climax when every generation returns to him and 'all is revealed'!

My spirit for every generation

'In the last days,' says the Lord, 'I will pour out my Spirit on all people. Your sons and daughters will prophesy, your young men will see visions, your old men will dream dreams. Even on my servants, both men and women, I will pour out my Spirit in those days.' (Acts 2: 17-18)

These are days that were partly fulfilled at Pentecost, but these are days that we are living in today; these are days that are opening up before us. We are this generation!

Sanballat asked, 'Can these stones come back to life from those heaps of rubble – burned as they are?' (Nehemiah 4:1-2). As we look around we may be tempted to ask the same. God is the best at rebuilding . . . read on and see what he is doing!

Prophetic words for the generations today

As I travel, in many nations I hear prophetic words spoken about the generations; I hear people catching God's vision and heart for each generation, sharing their thoughts and dreams. In this chapter, I have tried to capture the heart of what I have heard. This is not complete, it is not a word given to or by me, it is not the definitive statement, but rather the passion and heartbeat of what I have heard. Read this by the Spirit, read it and let yourself capture what I believe is an insight into the Word of God for each generation.

The older generation (approx. 50 years and over!)

Many have called this the Caleb generation. Caleb stayed true to God when others came back with a bad report; he stood and spoke boldly before all the generations.

God called him a man with a different spirit. He claimed the mountain for God. He stood up and spoke up boldly (Numbers 13:30).

I have heard this said of this generation many times, that they are a generation that have wanted the very best. They have stood through the tough times and are still standing. They have stood when few stood around them, they have kept the faith.

This generation is not second best, but the very best. They are a generation of champions and warriors, who can tell the stories of battles won. They have learned how to fight the good fight! They have learned how to fight and not faint.

Many feel that they are winding down, but what is still in front of them matters. They will proceed with a shout of triumph. They have not seen all that God has for them; there is more to come. What is before them matters; the past is training for what is still to come, for the victories of kings and princes.

Many have been hurt and disappointed, but these times will make them more effective, and the best is yet to come for those who have kept up the fight and stayed the course.

They are a generation that has not forgotten how to dream, through the good times and the bad. They dreamt when all around there was no hope. Their dreams were heaven sent; now is the time for them to hold out their hands to receive all that is coming to them.

It is time for them to leave the past and focus on the future. What has been was good in its season. This is a new season and God wants them to receive the challenge of stepping into the new. It is not the time to look back; it is the time to move forward.

This generation has been tested, so many have had prophetic promises that have not as yet come to pass. This has resulted in many of this generation feeling let down and betrayed. Many thought they would see these fulfilled in their youth, but God has his perfect timing, their dreams are not too late, they are not overdue. They are still their dreams but now is the time to look for them to come to life. Generations will know that it has not been by might, or by power but by God's Spirit that these things will now come to pass.

God wants to make a generation of fathers and mothers for the youth of the nations so that he can bring to pass these vision and dreams. He needs this generation to be as committed and involved as ever.

It is not the time to retire but the time to refire. It is the time for bodies to be renewed, for strength to be beyond the years and for energy to be released to accomplish all that they desire.

Many young adults are feeling discarded and abandoned; they desperately need someone older to adopt them and be parents to them. God is looking for a generation which will join with them, strengthen, encourage and love them, making themselves available and taking a prominent place in their lives, not by controlling them but through loving, prayerful support.

This generation will help to prepare the emerging leaders, opening their homes to the other generations. Inviting them in to receive and making preparation for their equipping and training. Many of this generation will spend most of their time preparing these coming leaders, pouring their lives into them. They will give them the strength of their years, the wisdom they have gained through the good times and the testing times.

This generation has seen the changes in the spirit; sometimes they feel that they will not be partakers of these changes, but they will see them quicker than they have seen any change in their lifetime.

The Lord is calling for this generation to take their stand as the fathers and mothers to a fatherless generation, which needs them and cannot wait They need them now. It is time for them to reach out and be there for this younger generation, to accept them, empower them and stand against everything that would look to attack them. This generation is to be their protection.

This is the time for generational gaps to be filled, to be there for the next generation. This must be the passion of this generation. There is a price that must be paid, but it is worth everything. There is a mandate on this generation to reach out and draw the next generation to its side and love them!

It is time for them to choose to commit, and sever their links with things that would hold them back. Time to let go of false ideas and restricted views of their future, time to be ready for change and be dependent on the Spirit of God. Many have said that this generation cannot change, but they will change by the Spirit of God. This generation will see the change as the fruit of their prayers and faithfulness.

This is not the generation who should feel that it is too late; they have an impact for today and a legacy to leave. It is time to run and do anything the other generations can do. It is the time to run and fight as never before. It is a time when the stamina that is a product of the past will be released into a sprint.

This generation will see the victories they have fought for; they will see the enemy under their feet.

Where times have been hard, where battles have been fought for days and even years they will see a release of victories, they will fight for the younger generation and win battles that they will not even be aware of. Their joy will be in seeing the liberation of their children and their children's children.

The middle generation (approx. 30-50 years of age)

I have heard it said several times that there is a Davidic anointing on this generation. They have zeal and a passion for God, like David. They will know how to raise their sons and prepare them for their destiny.

This generation has been described as a generation of champions who have the heart to see the nation return to God. They will love their nation as their predecessors did, but where their predecessors went to battle and saw many of their fellow warriors die, this generation will fight and live.

They are a praying generation who will be generous in

prayer and finances, which will be zealous in worship and intercession. They will take the night hours and pray until morning, they will make demands in the spirit that will be met even as they utter them.

The enemy has tried to destroy this generation but God has raised them up to take his kingdom to the ends of the earth. Problems will be seen as challenges, they will see the miracle before it is manifested. They will see the mountains moved, the walls fall and the ends of the earth liberated.

This is a generation that is coming into leadership; they are already leading in love, in service and giving. They will not wait for the office of leadership to be given to them, but they are already leading because of who they are. They have followers, who want to follow.

They will lead the generation before them and the generation to come. They stand in the gap and repair the breach of the generations. They will bring the old and the young together. They will see the best and be restorers of the breach. God is finding people who will hold and heal the wounds of the generations.

Their young will fight with them; they will learn how to raise their children as servants and soldiers of the most high God. They will not fear for them, but cheer them on as they move into the enemy's territory. They will know how to protect their little ones who are mighty in battle. They will know how to nurture them and raise a generation who run into the anointing. They will understand the times and the seasons for the young people and run with them. Like David they will prepare the way for their children, they will prepare a storehouse for them.

The younger generation (under 30 years of age)

Many have called this the Joshua generation; they are chosen to inherit the land. They will not wait for death, to come into their inheritance, but they will go and take their inheritance. Their inheritance is waiting for them. They will inherit what they have not looked or asked for. They will inherit what others have interceded for. They must remember that others have fought for and dreamed of what they will receive.

This is a consecrated generation for a high and noble task to rise up and possess the land, with an anointing for battle.

They will see things speed up, they will look and the answer will be there; they will speak and it will happen. They will see come to pass what many have spent years looking for. This will be normal to them; this will be their expectation.

There is an awakening sweeping across the earth; they will see what others have heard. This generation will see the glory of God poured out, they will see the streams in the desert, and they will see his glory poured out.

They will not live by the rules of previous generations. They will have a life and a vision that cannot be contained. They will look different . . . be different, with a power and zeal different from other generations. They will see what others have struggled to see. They will understand divine strategy in these days, and find it easy to walk in.

They will manifest as a wild radical generation of believers who practise holiness, who know how to love and forgive. They are an elite army, rising from every part of the earth. They are coming from the north, the south, the east and the west. They are rising up from the dry places, and emerging from the wilderness. They have been chosen for advance and not retreat.

They will take Jesus everywhere, into places of influence, to the poor and rich alike. They are a massive army being trained right now. There will not be time to train them later. Now is the time to equip and release them to be all they are called to be. They are called to be an army of prophets and prophetesses, to hear the beat of God's heart and march to its message, to stand in the city gates and prophesy.

This is the time for the spirit of the Nazarites. For the Elijah revolution. A radically obedient, holy generation full of grace, mercy and boldness.

There will be stadiums filled with youth praying, filled all over the world. They will come together for no other reason than to intercede and pray.

As they stay close to the anointed and as they serve them, God will open doors that they did not know existed. They will shake the nations and take his glory to the ends of the earth because they have a vision and passion for the harvest.

It will be understood why the enemy has tried to destroy them; he saw the end-time army, willing to die for what they believe, ready and willing to lay down their lives.

They have counted the cost of discipleship and moved on.

Previous generations have stood through hard times seeing little in return. They stood for this generation; they paid a price so that this generation could inherit.

All generations

God is calling all generations to love and honour each other. To work side by side, showing mercy and grace, love and compassion, laughing and crying together. Together they will stand against the culture of the world that wants to separate the generations.

As each generation takes its place, they will be an army that is invincible in the face of all opposition. Their weapons will complement each other, they will stand at the rear, support from the air, and advance from the front, but the greatest weapon of all will be their love.

This is the time for the Elijah spirit to prepare and open up the way. It is time for the curse to be broken off the nations.

Empowering a generation: the young people

Young people need the older generations to protect, encourage, understand and cheer them on. We need to be their greatest cheerleaders, dream big dreams with them and believe in them when the world seems to be tumbling around them.

Encourage them to dream dreams. The dreams that were given to Joseph seemed impossible. God will give this generation dreams that to us would seem as impossible as reaching the moon did to our forefathers. Today we can reach the moon, tomorrow their dreams can be reality.

They need those who will help them to realise their identity, and see the potential that is in them. When they are at the stage of discovering their identity they need our loving acceptance; when they want to take risks, they need us to be there through success or failure, still loving them and respecting them because they dared to go where we who move cautiously would fear to tread.

A generation must rise up and reverse the trend of leaving these young people without role models and the support and protection they deserve.

As the generation before them we can release them into the future. As Paul said to Timothy, 'Don't let anyone despise your youth, but be an example in speech, word and deed' (1 Timothy 4:12). It would seem to me that the generation which would despise him would be those older than himself. Let's give them our trust.

Encourage the young men to be self-controlled. In everything set them an example by doing what is good. In your teaching show integrity, seriousness and soundness of speech that cannot be condemned, so that those who oppose you may be ashamed because they have nothing bad to say about us. (Titus 2:6-8)

It is so easy to point the finger at young people, to enter into needless arguments. We are called to set them an example, and to be careful in our speech towards them, fully trusting them. There is nothing like trust to provoke trust.

The teaching of God is attractive, Jesus was attractive, and every generation followed him. Our lives need to be attractive to the teenagers of today. Sadly, I see so often that they do not want to be a part of church as portrayed by those older than themselves.

A visiting pastor came to a small group in my home church where every generation was present. At the end he prayed, 'Lord, forgive me that I thought this generation of young people were looking for gimmicks, I now see that they are looking for relationship.'

So many of them lack good fathers and mothers that they can turn to. The Body of Christ has an army of them if they will be mobilised!

One of the saddest things I see and hear is the expectation that during teenage years there will be a breakdown in family relationships. I am not disagreeing that they need other relationships in their lives. There is nothing in the Word of God that leads us to beliee that where Jesus is at the centre of the home there should be any 'teenage rebellion'.

Our young people need as many godly heroes as they can get, they need many godly relationships, but they still need their parents.

I see a growing number of teenagers coming into ministry with their parents; I see them taking their place alongside their parents, becoming part of the 'family firm!'

My youngest two children are currently 18 and 16 years of age. They are part of all I do; they gladly take responsibility and make the necessary sacrifices; we are friends as we travel. They are free to fly, free to find what God has for them and one day they may move into another arena that God has for them, but meanwhile we take the kingdom together!

What faith do we have for them? What vision do we have for families? Teenage years are good years, they are years of change, but then so is every stage of development. They can grow in family perfectly connected, and in secure relationship.

The challenge is to support and release them into all that God has for them. They will be wild for Jesus, they will be radical and they need us to accept them just as they are and not rein them in when God is breaking them loose.

One generation thought it found the fullness of freedom in Christ, then the next generation found another level, and still that freedom is being explored. 'The Call' event that occurred in Washington saw thousands of disorganised young people sold out for Jesus. They are expressing what I long to have. I want to be part of it and through relationship with them I shall be. If we do not hold onto relationship with them, we will be excluded! If we disconnect from them there will be a missing generation, and we will compound the fractured generations instead of being instruments of healing and reconciliation.

I travel to countries where I see teenagers whose bodies are mutilated because they have stood for the name of Jesus, their friends have been martyred, their families lost, and still they are militant in advancing against the darkness around them. Nothing, not even death would stand in their way. I spoke to some of them, I saw them, and they became my heroes. Such a young man was Daniel.

> Then the king ordered Ashpenaz . . . to bring in some of
> the Israelites from the royal family and the nobility –

young men without any physical defect, handsome, showing aptitude for every kind of learning, well informed,
quick to understand and qualified to serve in the king's
palace . . . Daniel resolved not to defile himself [by eating
food given to gods] . . . .To these four young men God
gave knowledge and understanding of all kinds of litera-
ture and learning. And Daniel could understand visions
and dreams of all kinds. (Daniel 1:3-17)

A word to the young people

You are generation-gap fillers. Paul said to Timothy, 'Don't let
anybody despise your youth but be an example.' It isn't going
to be easy to stand in the gap but the challenge is laid out in
Paul's word to Timothy. You are called to be an example to
the other generations by the way you live.

Live your lives being holy and pure, so that the children can
see the way to go; reach out a hand to them, be their heroes.

Be radical for the sake of the older generations, you are our
prophetic vision. You like the latest fashions and music, you
also like to go beyond the boundaries that so many of the
older generations have fallen into through religion.

Stir us up but don't leave us out!

Forgive us when we have despised your youth, but please
don't despise our wisdom.

Listen to your father, who gave you life, and do not
despise your mother when she is old . . . The father of a
righteous man has great joy; he who has a wise son
delights in him. May your father and mother be glad,
may she who gave you birth rejoice! (Proverbs 23:22-25)

Will you work with us to be restorers of the breach, and fulfil the prayer of Jesus 'that they may be one' and the generational fractures in the precious Body of Jesus healed?

Rescuing a generation: the children

Our children are part of this whole generational flow and will be impacted by it, either for good or for ill. The generation of children belong to all of us and we are commissioned to take responsibility for them whether we have children of our own or not. Our first responsibility is to our own children and then, with them, to make a difference to children who are not our birth children.

We all have a calling and a destiny to impact the youngest generation. We are responsible for the world they live in today, for the laws that are passed, for the society they are born into.

They are killing each other in schools; they are having babies before they have left childhood. They are shot and wounded in war, die in famine and grow up not knowing that there is a Saviour who loves them and died for them.

There is a battle for this generation. Many die before they even begin to fulfil their destiny, they are killed through abortion. Child sacrifice is still in the nations, many are sold into prostitution or thrown into rubbish bins, sexual abuse is rampant, and families are torn apart.

The Enemy knows the strategies of God better than we do sometimes. He knows that if he can destroy a child he has taken their adulthood and affected the generations that will follow them. When he kills a child he stems the generational flow. When he destroys their childhood he understands that he destroys the rest of their lives, and the lives of their children too.

It is time that a generation rose up on their behalf. This is not a task that can be completed by a few, it is the responsibility of the other generations to defend, protect, rescue, restore and empower them to be all that they were called to be before the foundation of the world. (Ephesians 1:3-4)

We are agents of change. It is time for our generation to rise up on their behalf, cry out to God and go and rescue them from the hands of the evil one. None of us is exempt from this call, 'A generation for a generation.'

There are children of destiny that the enemy is trying to destroy. He tried to destroy Moses and Jesus by killing the children of their generation. Samuel's mother had to fight for his birth.

Every child and young person has a destiny, every child has an anointing, and for every single child God has a purpose and a plan. When you see a child that is the sickest, the naughtiest, the poorest, when you see a child with problems ranged around them, the tendency is to recoil, instead of recognising what is happening and rising up on their behalf. Grasp that child, with all the love you can give, fight evil with prayer, fasting and love to deliver that child. That is a commission that God has given each one of us, none of us are exempt.

One generation can turn the tide of evil for another; one generation can enter the enemy's camp and take another generation back.

In nations that have some respect for children they do not send the children to war, the older generation fights to protect the land for their future. So it must be in the kingdom, one generation fighting, rescuing and taking the land from the enemy and raising children in the kingdom.

One generation will be asked about the next generation and what inheritance they left them.

Kenneth Copeland had an outlook that we should all share regarding children:

'Brother Copeland, I don't have any children,' someone said to him.

'Yes you do. Everyone has children. They are all around you. They are on the streets. They are in your church. They are such a large part of our society that they affect everything we do. Begin to pray for an outpouring of God on the children around you. This is God's time for the children.'

This is harvest time among the young people. Every time you hear of violence regarding children on the television, say out loud, 'Our children are taught of the Lord and great is the anointing and peace on them. AMEN' (see Isaiah 54:13).

The children are our generation of children, we must all love them; we must all pray for them; we must win them, disciple them and support them as they 'Go into all the world'.

Custodians of a generation

I used to have a problem trying to understand how God could have entrusted Jesus to parents that left him in Jerusalem! Then, one day, I understood. It wasn't a weakness, it was a manifestation of strength in the way Mary and Joseph brought him up.

They ensured that Jesus was raised in the loving inclusive community of God. If parents take their children out with friends and other families, that is the time they relax because the children are interacting with others. That is how Mary and Joseph began to go around asking where Jesus was before they realised that he was with none of them and had stayed in Jerusalem.

This is the environment that God is wanting for children. Children do not belong in an environment that is not their foundational place. Their foundational place is within the community of the Body of Christ. We are all responsible to and for them, to have our hearts pure and holy towards them and to fast, pray for and reach the generation of children around us.

Today, the prophetic word is that God is doing a supernatural work in this generation; he will birth revival among them. In every nation people show me words of prophecy they have been given, tell me about a message they have heard, or a vision they have had. They all have the same message: the Holy Spirit is moving in a powerful way among children and young people on the earth.

The rest of us can get on board, help stir those flames and light those fires to see revival in our day.

In recognising who God has called us to be in these young lives, we must first catch his heart and vision for them. He has great plans for them, he has entrusted them to us and we must enlarge our own hearts to catch the heart of God for the children of the nations.

We can accept them as a precious gift and say with Jacob (Genesis 33:5), 'These are the children God has graciously given your servant, bring them to me that I may bless them.'

If every child who had given their life to Jesus over the last 25 years were still active for the kingdom where would the church be today? We would have a mighty army.

It takes a generation to raise a generation, to nurture and protect them. Part of this answer I believe is in restoring the generational flow to them. We have dismantled this and abandoned children to their peers. God knows best how to protect and nurture his little ones; he placed them in the generations within family, and in the generational community of God.

Education is passed on and developed from generation to generation. The professor nurtures a younger man who, in turn, will do the same and so it is with the Kingdom, with the

preparation of the bride of Christ, with the developing army that will fulfil the great commission.

We are custodians of what has been given to us, but it is also for the children. As God said to Abraham and to Moses, 'I am giving you this, but it is also for your children, for their children, for your descendants' (Deuteronomy 6).

The only thing we leave of eternal value on this earth is the next generation!

Faith for the youngest generation

Even John Wesley realised that his vision for children was too limited because he wrote:

> I began meeting with the children in the afternoon though with little hopes of doing them any good; but I had not long spoken on their natural state before many of them were in tears, and five or six so affected, that they could not refrain from crying aloud to God. When I began praying, their cries increased, so that my voice was soon lost. (John Wesley, 30 July 1759)

Despite his initial limited vision, John Wesley realised the necessity of impacting the next generation. He set aside time for them.

We need great men of God to be there for the children. The children are the future; they will take the anointing to the next generation. Otherwise all that we are will die with us.

We need to dream big dreams with them and raise our faith for them. I was leading a prayer meeting in my home church, and there was one little boy who had been left by his mother for somebody to look after until she could return to collect him. I was speaking and said, 'We must have faith to believe that our children could even die for Jesus. Have you got that faith, that your children could be so strong that, if it came to it, they would even lay down their lives to death for Jesus?'

On hearing this the boy jumped up and began to tell us of

the things that he had suffered as he stood up for Jesus at school. The whole place went quiet and we listened to his testimony. We must renew our faith and vision for what God can do with our children. He can do more than we have dreamed.

As we respect them and what the Holy Spirit is wanting to release through them, so we will also raise a generation of children who respect the other generations; they, in turn, will command the respect of those who will come after them.

God had refused to deliver the children of Israel from Egypt until every man woman and child could leave together.

> Then fear came upon them and they grumbled to God saying, 'Our wives and our children will be taken as plunder. Wouldn't it be better for us to go back to Egypt?' And they said to each other, 'We should choose a leader and go back to Egypt.' (Numbers 14:3-4)

As our faith rises it will protect our children. Generally they are more affected by our fear than by circumstances.

Don't underestimate this generation. If you do, then they'll underestimate themselves. Tell them what they are worth, what they can stand for, what their potential is. Tell them what Jesus can do through them; give them a challenge and they will rise to it.

Sometimes I hear adults say, 'Lord, send us revival, send us revival.' I say, 'Why don't you go to where God is lighting the fire? He is lighting a fire over there amongst the children, he's lighting the fires amongst the young people. If you want revival, go and fan God's fires instead of calling down your own.'

Everywhere I go people give me words of prophecy they have received, tell me about a message they heard or a vision they have had. They all have one message; the Holy Spirit is moving in a powerful way among the children and young people on earth.

The rest of us can get on board, help stir those flames and light those fires to see revival in our day.

As we receive life and 'revelation', so often we look to share with our peers. This has its place, but the Scriptures repeat the command to pass these things on to our children.

> What other nation is so great as to have their gods near them the way the Lord our God is near us whenever we pray to him? . . . Only be careful, and watch yourselves closely so you do not forget the things your eyes have seen or let them slip from your heart as long as your live. Teach them to your children and to their children after them. (Deuteronomy 4:7-9)

Moses spoke with passion, and cautioned the people to be careful and watch themselves closely, to not forget or let things slip from their heart for the whole of their lives. This caution needs to be heeded. When we forget, the next generation is robbed; when we withhold we keep from them the treasures that have been entrusted to us.

Moses was speaking to all Israel, he did not take those who had children of their own on one side, he was speaking to everyone. Our minds and hearts need to be renewed to consider this command, and to begin to live it out.

> The secret things belong to the Lord our God, but the things revealed belong to us and to our children for ever, that we may follow all the words of this law. (Deuteronomy 29:29)

We rob the next generation when we do not give them what is rightly theirs. The things revealed to us are not ours alone, they belong to our children too.

> The Lord said, 'Abraham will surely become a great and powerful nation, and all nations on earth will be blessed through him. For I have chosen him, so that he will direct his children and his household after him to keep the way

of the Lord by doing what is right and just, so that the Lord will bring about for Abraham what he has promised him.' (Genesis 18:18-19)

God was entrusting Abraham with the destiny of his people. That trust was intrinsically bound up with his attitude to his God and to his children. His love of God meant that he was prepared to sacrifice his son and as a result he was told:

Your descendants will take possession of the cities of their enemies, and through your offspring all nations on earth will be blessed. (Genesis 22:17-18)

God needed a way of fulfilling his promise to Abraham. That way was through the faithfulness of Abraham directing his children and his household after him to keep the way of the Lord. Thus the Lord would bring about for Abraham what he had promised. Through the next generation the promises will be fulfilled and perpetuated on the earth.

Romans 9:8 tells us, 'It is the children of promise who are regarded as Abraham's offspring.'

That brings the responsibility to all of us. Abraham was faithful in passing on to the next generation; Jewish people have ways to pass on their heritage within their lifestyle; we need to reclaim our roots and re-establish our responsibility to the Lord and to our children.

In the Book of Acts, homes were the meeting place where the generations were mobilised together – parents with their children, single people as their friends and all experiencing the miracle-working power of God. Children are secure in extended families. They need others in their lives who will love them unconditionally. Their peers can never give them the security and safety they need to flourish and grow.

Many children have Christian homes, but many parents are struggling, and children need others in their lives as well as the parents.

Our responsibility to the next generation is also manifest in the way we support their parents.

I believe what God wants is to see parents discipling their children in the way described in Deuteronomy 6. Then, as a body, we take these children and we enable them to go out and reach the lost with us. We take them as an army to go out and reach the unsaved, we rise up with them and together take our responsibility to win families for Jesus.

Discipling the youngest generation

Our lives are a living example to the next generation. In this chapter we are considering the commission of Jesus to 'make disciples of all nations'. This calls for proactive discipleship of every generation. Sometimes this is called 'fathering', the name does not matter, the outcome does!

This chapter is about the discipleship of children. By 'discipleship' I mean the lifestyle that Jesus showed us. He lived with, walked beside, communicated, sent out, received back, loved unconditionally, validated and rebuked, modelled for and trusted those he was investing his life in. He showed us how to disciple effectively so that the ends of the earth would be reached.

Deuteronomy 6:4-9 gives a very clear picture of discipleship of the youngest generation:

> The Lord our God, the Lord is one. Love the Lord your God with all your heart and with all your soul and with all your strength. These commandments that I give you today are to be upon your hearts. Impress them on your children. Talk about them when you sit at home and when you walk along the road, when you lie down and when you get up. Tie them as symbols on your hands and bind them on your foreheads. Write them on the door frames of your houses and on your gates.

Verse 20 says, 'In the future when your son asks you . . . tell him.' This is just what Jesus did with his disciples. It was a lifestyle relationship. So we have to consider who could have this type of relationship best with a child. Surely this must be the parent! As they often live with the child their role is automatically one of discipleship.

Children see them in their work, recreation, ministry, at home, within the Body, their prayer life, in their relationships: everywhere children are silent observers. They were created to absorb all that we do. Take time to look at your whole life through the eyes of a child!

My dream is that a generation of parents rises up to once again become the primary disciplers of their children.

Generally they have abdicated this responsibility to the church and the end result is that children are not receiving all that God intended them to receive. We end up losing children. Abraham was found faithful in raising his son and the Lord said, 'I have chosen him so that he will direct his children.' Through this faithfulness the promises of God would be fulfilled for his, and future generations.

The environment of discipleship

Everyone disciples their children. How often has it been said, 'You are just like your mum/dad'? The parents did not tell the child that they had to grow up like them. They just did through the natural family dynamics of modelling, experience and communication!

Your natural family is where you received your values, where your character and world view were formed. A peer environment is excellent for receiving cognitive knowledge; that's why schools are excellent because we can input knowledge and information in that environment. Most of what shapes who you are has been gained from an intergenerational environment called your family.

So, parents are the filters for the children. Through the parents their character, world-view and values are formed. Through them they understand the character of and relationship with their Heavenly Father. Just as their father forgives them, so their Abba forgives them; just as their mother meets their needs, so will their Abba; just as my parents love me unconditionally so my Heavenly Father loves me.

Sadly, this filter has been marred. All parents have sinned and fallen short of the glory of God, and so the image of God has been marred in the soul of every child.

If a child is taken to secular counselling because of problems, they are always seen in the context of the family. We need to restore this dynamic to the Body of Christ so that healing comes in the context of their family. So often the family is always separated with little or no opportunity for children to be with their parents.

Most adults automatically pass on to their children the things that are important to them. Parents take their sons to soccer, their daughters to dancing classes and they encourage their children to become musicians. Whatever they consider of value they impart to their children. So it is with the things of the kingdom. All these things are good, they can help to develop gifts and skills in the children, but there may be things of eternal significance which are totally excluded from a parent's relationship with the child.

We focus on passing on an inheritance in the natural world but what about the things that are going to last for eternity in the life of your child?

I am sometimes asked when it is possible for people to start discipling their children. The answer I give is, 'They can start the moment they are born again.' When someone comes to Jesus it is often said, 'Go and tell someone what Jesus has done for you.' If we could just change that one statement and say to people who have children, 'Go and tell your children what has just happened to you,' then at that moment discipleship would begin and we would begin to envision that child.

Every time somebody with children comes to you with a story or a testimony, please say to them, 'Have you told your children?' This will begin to change the culture in the Body of Christ and you will start the natural biblical role of discipleship. I believe this is one of the foundational commands of God and one of the foundations to restore for the next generation.

Too long this has been ignored.

Jesus said, 'If you love me, keep my commandments.' Love him with all your heart and you will find it easy to tell your children!

The parent connection!

Parents have the anointing to be the greatest ministers their children could ever have. They are God-designed to be the best!

Sadly, what has happened is that the Church has tried to take the role for them, yet at the same time wishing the parents would do it. Parents feel inadequate, ill-equipped, and generally lack confidence.

We are called to disciple our own children till the day we die, though the dynamics will change as the children get older.

There are certain basic requirements to release this dynamic of generational discipleship:

Honour the office of parenthood

The office of parenthood needs to be respected and honoured in a new way. Sometimes it is looked down on, as if being a parent will give a bias, or bad judgement. When parents come apologetically to me with something to say about their children, I say to them, 'Sit down, tell me everything. You know your child best and I want to hear from you. If you don't speak up for your child who will!' They look shocked, because the message that is commonly given is that parents are 'biased'. And so they should be!

If a child from a non-Christian family is prevented from coming to church, we grumble about the parent. I would not let my children go to something I did not agree with. This could be a sign of good parenting.

Parenthood is a holy, God-given role and should not be abused. As we restore it to its highest place, and stand in awe of it, I believe we will start to release blessing.

Jesus did not over-ride parents. He respected that God anointed them for their children in a very special way.

When Jairus came to him on behalf of his daughter, Jesus took the parents into the room when he raised her up. He put others out of the room, but he included and honoured the parents.

We must restore an honouring of this position. Whether the parents are Christians or not, the office is God-given. As we empower, include and honour parents we will release the anointing of God on their lives, and on the lives of their children. Instead of trying to do the parents' job for them by taking on their role of discipleship, we could focus on envisioning, praying for and equipping them.

Fight for your children

> The Royal official asked, 'Sir, come down before my little child is dead.' So Jesus answered, 'Go in peace. Your son will live.' (John 4:49-50)

> One of the throng said, 'I have brought my son to you,' and with tears he said, 'Lord, I believe. Constantly help my weakness of faith . . .' Jesus took a strong grip on his hand and lifted him up.' (Mark 9:17, 24, 27; Amplified)

When we come on behalf of our children as these fathers did, Jesus acts.

He wants us to rise up strong on their behalf; when we are weak expect him to help, when we don't know what to say it is all right to be inarticulate. When we are upset it is all right to cry as we come to him. He wants to act on our children's behalf; he has entrusted them to us and expects us to come to him on their behalf.

> When she could hide him no longer, she got a papyrus basket for him and coated it with tar and pitch and put him among the reeds. (Exodus 2:3)

Moses was protected by a mother who refused to surrender his life, and by a diligent older sister who watched over him.

Hannah fought for the conception of her child, Samuel, when she cried,

> Remember me, and do not forget your servant but give me a son, then I will give him to the Lord. (1 Samuel 1:11)

When God gave her the child she had asked for, she continued to take spiritual authority over his life.

> I prayed for this child, and the Lord has granted me what I asked of him. So now I give him to the Lord. For his whole life he shall be given over to the Lord. (1 Samuel 1:27-28)

Samuel was surrendered to God, and other desires took second place. How Hannah must have longed to nurture him and watch him grow. She had waited so long for her son, but she put her child's godly destiny first.

The mother of the sons of Zebedee came to Jesus on behalf of her sons and Jesus never reprimanded her for so doing.

One of the things that God is going to do in these next few years is to restore to parents the primary role of disciplers to their children.

I believe this is the heartbeat of God. I am not contradicting the fact that we are all responsible for the next generation, many children have no Christian homes, many parents are struggling, and children need others in their lives as well as their parents. But parents have a specific and unique calling. I believe that when we stand before the throne of God he is going to ask us about the children. Parents will be asked about the greatest ministry they were given, their children.

I have a vision of a church where the attention is turned to the parents. Where they support, equip and resource parents to be the primary disciplers of their children. A church where this role is seen to be of at least equal importance to the role that currently exists with children. Then we will start to empower parents to raise soldiers, and the church will be able to take these soldiers, and make them into an army to win the lost.

Let's raise up a generation of outward looking children who know that the point of being church is to equip us to fulfil the great commission.

Fathers

The impact of fathers taking up their godly role can be measured in the lives of their own children, their children's children, other children around them and their spiritual children.

Today the role of fathering is being restored to the body of Christ. So many are looking for spiritual fathers and mothers. When fathers are spiritual fathers to their own children a wonderful integration takes place. The children receive wholeness in their growth.

Men and women are being raised up to be spiritual parents to younger men and women in the faith. This is truly marvellous and I am in that role myself. It is imperative that we nurture others. However I believe that God requires us to be accountable for discipling our own children at the same time.

This role is so important. Fathers help their children discover their identity; they are their security, provider, strength and confidant. Just as they provide an earthly inheritance for their children in the same way they establish a spiritual inheritance.

Job took his responsibility seriously (Job 1:5). He rose early every morning to offer a sacrifice for his sons. Eli was rebuked for not training his sons, and so are we today:

> Fathers, do not irritate and provoke your children to anger but raise them tenderly in the training, discipline, counsel and admonition of the Lord. (Ephesians 6:4)

> For the grave cannot thank you. Death cannot praise you. Those who go down to the pit cannot hope for your truth. The living, the living, they shall praise you, as I do to this day. The father shall make known your truth to his children. (Isaiah 38:18-19)

Here is a declaration of thanks and of praise to God, building up to a climax. The grave cannot do it – people who are dead cannot do it – nobody can praise or thank him enough. Only those who are living can give praise on this earth.

Then the climax: 'The father shall make known your truth to his children.' This is the father's offering of praise, his offering of thanks to the almighty God, making known God's truth to his children so that they pass it on to their children.

When a parent looks at the small baby in their arms they tremble at the responsibility given to them, but they learn how to parent by making a decision to do the best they can. They watch others, ask for advice, read books, attend classes do everything they can to discover how they can be the best. But eventually it is by actual parenting, when the baby is born that they learn the most. So it is with spiritual parenting. The quiet voice of the Holy Spirit will direct us, others can help us but we learn as we go along!

> Sons are a heritage from the Lord, children a reward from him. Like arrows in the hands of a warrior are sons born in one's youth. Blessed is the man whose quiver is full of

them. They will not be put to shame when they contend with their enemies in the gate. (Psalm 127:3-5)

Fathers have an inheritance in their children; they are given as a reward. They are their prize, their joy, and most precious possession. A generation takes its role as warriors for the kingdom when they take these arrows (our children) and 'aim them' in the right direction, so that when the day comes to release them they will fly right towards the target, taking the nations and winning battles against the powers of darkness because they were aimed in the right direction in the hands of their father.

Fathers will cheer as they see their children walk through the gates of their enemies and take the land.

Here is the promise outlined in Psalm 25:12-13:

> Who is the man who reverently fears the Lord? He will instruct him in the way he has chosen for him. He will spend his days in prosperity, and his descendants will inherit the land.

Grandparents

> Children's children are a crown to the aged and parents are the pride of their children. (Proverbs 17:6)

What a generational glory. Grandparents seeing their grandchildren as a crown to them, their jewels bright, parents proud of their older parents, children proud of their parents. This is how God sees it; how he created the family of generations to be.

With every child God gives the anointing to parent them, and as we nurture them we nurture the generations that will follow, when we nurture our grandchildren so we sow into the lives of their children too. No wonder God holds us responsible for so great a task.

61

There is no vision here of generational gaps, of teenagers not being able to get on with their parents, of grandparents being put on one side.

Let's renew our mind with God's way of seeing things; let's change our expectations and expect to see our generations God's way.

On goes the throne of God throughout the generations! His dominion is protected and the plans and purposes of his heart fulfilled.

The returning prodigal children

This is the season for the return of the prodigals, for killing the fatted calf and holding celebrations! The spirit of Elijah is around!

I speak to many despondent parents whose children have taken their inheritance and left. This is the time to dream dreams, to renew hope. 'Faith is the evidence of things hoped for.' When hope is taken away then the evidence, which is faith, disappears.

In the last few months I have seen the fruit of praying parents – children are returning.

While you pray for and wait for your own children, sow into the lives of other children. Continue to bear fruit and be an instrument of healing to the generation of your child.

Being together

I sometimes hear parents say, 'I cannot worship God if I've got my children with me.' I say to them, 'If you have small children, you can't sleep all night. If you have small children, you can't go shopping like you used to. If you have small children, you probably haven't the money you used to have. It's

62

for a period of your life and you take that as being a part of having children. It is a part of the blessing of being responsible for your children.

'So, if you cannot worship God in the same way as you did before you had children, it's a period in your life that Jesus expects you to make some adjustments in order to accommodate your children. Just as you do in other areas of your life.'

Let's get back to being normal. We have all these religious ideas that come along and rob us of the joy that could be ours in seeing our children minister, worship, pray, give and receive and win the lost within the context of church life.

We need to worship together just as they did in biblical times, and just as many other religions still do today. This is a period in your life when they need to see you operating in the church. A respected leader told me once that he grew up thinking that ministry was only given, not received because he never saw his parents receiving.

You can have the extra blessing and come to a higher place as you worship God with your children. Don't always give someone else this privilege when it has been given to you! This is preparation for the day when we will all be worshipping around the throne together.

In every area of our lives there is sacrifice. I have sacrificed for my children but I love my children and I wouldn't give up one bit of that sacrifice because it is actually my greatest joy. I would not want to pass that to anyone else. It is mine, given by God to me.

Don't ask what the church is doing for your children ask how the church can better equip you!

Generally churches are struggling in children's ministry; they are short of workers and are consumed with trying to meet the needs of children from Christian families. I am certainly not speaking against children's ministry; I have been part of it myself, but I do think this is a time of change. There is a lost and dying world of children who cannot be reached because manpower is not being used in the right way.

D. L. Moody would not let children from Christian families go to Sunday school because he said it would stop parents discipling their children. It did!

God is calling every fathering heart to rise up and reach out to the children. However I believe that it is an abomination in the eyes of God if we seek to father, or promote the fathering of others when our own birth children are not being fathered.

The very heartbeat of God is in the fathering of our own children and from there we restore the nations, from there we can father others, from there a generation will rise up who have been fathered themselves and who themselves will father generations and be nation takers.

Abraham was proved first in his love and devotion to his own son; he then became the father of nations.

When a generation of parents and grandparents, when a whole preceding generation takes on the discipleship or fathering of the next a new destiny is released. They will know how to father the one coming after them. We could be the generation that releases fathering into the generations.

Bridging the gap

Deuteronomy 4:2, 9-10

When the commands of God were given to the people of Israel, they were given a command with the commands. In Deuteronomy Moses speaks to the people:

> . . . keep the commands of the Lord your God that I give you.

> Only take heed to yourself and diligently keep yourself lest you forget the things your eyes have seen, and lest they depart from your heart all the days of your life; teach them to your children and your grandchildren. Especially concerning the day you stood before the Lord your God in Horeb, when the Lord said to me, 'Gather the people to me and I will let them hear my words, that they may learn to fear me all the days that they live upon the earth, and that they may teach their children.' (Amplified Bible)

This command is repeated many times in the book of Deuteronomy; it was an integral part of the giving of the law, a vital part of its application. One generation, as fathers, was told by God to write his commands on their own hearts, to let them become life, and then out of that life to tell their children.

Malachi 4:4-6

This text starts with 'Remember Horeb . . .' reminding us of the commands that God had given, and how we should pass them on, but he then goes on to say, 'See, I will send you Elijah, the prophet, before the coming of the great and dreadful day of the Lord, and he will turn the hearts of the fathers to the children and the hearts of the children to the fathers, lest I come and strike the land with a curse.'

The word 'see' or 'behold' seems to suggest that it is linked to the previous verse.

God knew a day was coming when he was going to have to do a supernatural work in order that the flow of his command as at Horeb between the fathers and sons (generation to generation) could be restored. He said he would send the spirit of Elijah!

This is the spirit that is on the earth today. That is why this message is being received, as never before; why God is getting our attention about the youngest generation and challenging us to respond.

Once more the hearts of the fathers are being turned to the children: natural fathers, spiritual fathers, fathers of nations and fathers of the generations are being turned. As the hearts of the fathers turn, as they become the initiators, so the hearts of the children will respond.

The final statement in Malachi 4:6 says '. . . or else I will come and strike the land with a curse.' The result of restoring fathering to the children and across the generations is freedom from the curse for our nation. The message is significant for our families and for the generations around us but is also redemptive for the land. These are days when God is moving in power, not just in the church but also across the nation. This message can change the destiny of your nation, and release blessing instead of the curse.

Now is the time to rise up and be all you were called to be, firstly for your children, but also for other children, for the younger women, for the young men, for your spiritual sons and daughters and for the generations around you, and so impact the nations.

The Old Testament finishes with this promise in Malachi and the New Testament begins with:

> This is the genealogy of Jesus Christ the son of David, the son of Abraham . . . Thus there were fourteen generations from Abraham to David, fourteen from David to the exile to Babylon and fourteen from the exile to the Christ. (Matthew 1:1, 17)

Forty-two generations, flowing one from the other until their final glory in the birth of the Son of God who came to take away the sin of the world!

He is the Author and Finisher, sending the Spirit of Elijah to restore again that perfect relational flow until one generation walks right into the throne room of God and the generations reach their final destiny.

Ezekiel 22:30

When there is disunity or lack of relationship between the generations we often talk about having generation 'gaps'. The answer to 'gaps' is found in Ezekiel 22:30:

> I sought for a man who would build up the wall and stand before me in the gap on behalf of the land, so I would not have to destroy it, but I found none.

If we take Ezekiel 22:30 and overlay it with Malachi 4:5-6 we can see that they flow together. God is looking for people who will stand before him 'in the gap', who will intercede and reach out across the gaps, no matter how far they are stretched in doing so. People who will reach out a hand and be instruments of reconciliation 'on behalf of the land', so that he will not have to 'strike the land with a curse'.

Remember the cross and Jesus' wounded body? What did that do to your heart? It brought you to the cross, where you were redeemed, where you were purchased with the precious blood of Jesus and made whole. So why are we, as the Body of Christ, still walking around fractured and broken? We are his body. This is about Jesus. He is calling us to be healers of the generations so that his precious Body might walk in that perfect wholeness.

I have chosen to be one of those people to stand in the gap (any age can stand in the gap). Children are great bridges between the generations. Could this be one of the reasons we are told to be like them? Who will pray and, in love, reach out and bring healing and reconciliation in the homes, churches, neighbourhoods and nations?

> Those who are among you shall build up the old waste places. You shall raise up the foundations of many generations. You shall be called the repairer of the breach, the restorer of streets to dwell in. (Isaiah 58:12)

From generation to generation: Judges 2:10

> When this generation had returned to its fathers a generation grew up who did not know their God.

This simple verse could be a key in helping us to understand how and why spiritual as well as relational breakdown happens between generations. If one generation does not know God, then the generation before must hold some responsibility. I am not offering simplistic answers or even suggesting that these are the only ones but in looking at this situation the following is something of what I have discovered:

A generation was growing up without strong spiritual leadership

The background of this time was that there was a huge spiritual vacuum over the nation. The Temple had not been built, and the Tabernacle not frequented by everyone. God did not ask that Joshua raise up a leader from his sons and forbade the High Priests to be leaders, as with Moses and Aaron. Only to Jesus has been given both government and priesthood.

Previous generations had known the presence of God on their leaders, as had been when 'the Lord exalted Joshua in the sight of all Israel, and they revered him all the days of his life, just as they had revered Moses (Joshua 4:14).

There was an absence of signs and wonders

It was said of Moses, 'For no one has ever shown the mighty power and awesome deeds Moses did in the sight of all Israel. (Deuteronomy 34:12)

The generation of Moses grew up seeing the mighty hand of God, they knew his awesome power and because they had seen it they knew their God was unique, that there was no other like him. They had seen his hand of deliverance. They knew their God. He was their hero!

What other nation is so great as to have their gods near them the way the Lord our God is near us whenever we pray to him? (Deuteronomy 4:7)

Moses reminded them of the importance of their children not only seeing for themselves, but of knowing what God had done for their forefathers.

Remember today that your children were not the ones who saw and experienced the discipline of the Lord your God: his majesty, his mighty hand, his outstretched arm; the signs he performed and the things he did in the heart of Egypt . . . (Deuteronomy 11:2-3a)

God had performed the signs and wonders as a heritage for their children. During the time of Joshua they saw the sun stand still, they saw the waters 'cut off and stand in a heap'

(Joshua 3:13). But after Joshua a generation grew up without the manifest power of God.

Jesus preached with signs following, his Word was accompanied by signs and miracles. He was a living manifest epistle, he was the Word.

When Stephen spoke before the Sanhedrin (Acts 7) he recounted what God had done 400 years previously! He was showing the continuity of Messiah, recounting the marvellous deeds and giving them the context of their own history. History declares his deeds among the people!

A generation needs to recount the wonders of God to the next, bringing the story right up to date. Stories of the mighty hand of God at work, stories of personal deliverance, stories of the nation's deliverance, stories of the families' deliverance, stories that can be passed on from generation to generation.

> Make known among the nations what he has done. (Psalm 105:1)

> How great are his signs, how mighty his wonders. His kingdom is an eternal kingdom: his dominion endures from generation to generation. (Daniel 4:3)

This causes us to ask where the signs and wonders are for our generation and for our children and what impact this has had on the coming generation who are looking for 'spiritual experiences'.

At the beginning of their ministry, T. L. and Daisy Osborne who have travelled the nations with the Gospel, cried out to God for miracles, signs and wonders. They searched relentlessly until they could be in the presence of those who could 'show them how'. They have now impacted the world. They have generations following after them.

Children and young people (and adults) need the Word and experience to line up. When experience does not line up with the Word most will believe the experience.

As we catch the heart of God for restoration, let's cry out, fast, pray, walk in holiness and reach out for signs and wonders. Jesus had all ages following him, they could sit with him all day, they heard what he said and they saw the signs that followed.

When we walk and speak with the demonstration of the power of God, a mighty explosion takes place that leaves an indelible mark on every generation.

When I return to my Father I look forward to seeing him and saying, 'After me is coming a generation that knows their God!' This is the vision that keeps me going.

Discovering and keeping

The seed

I recently spent a week under the ministry of a well-known evangelist who is still travelling the nations and winning souls at the age of 77. His passion to pass on to the younger generations was so inspirational. When he saw the children he said, 'This is what I came for!'

As I read one of his books the lifestyle of discipleship within his own family and the younger generations around him was like a blazing trail.

His book, *T. L. Osborn: Tragedy, Trauma, Triumph* is a tribute to his dear wife Daisy who died in 1995. Their grandson Tommy O'Dell writes:

> As a young boy I thought she [Daisy, his grandmother] was an angel incarnate, her house was where angels lived. Her spirit gave light to my life. She was precious to me . . . She was there when my brain was burned out and there was no hope for me . . . she fasted and interceded on my behalf as my mother did. When I was left for dead, Jesus came to me and healed me. My Grandmother's legacy is incalculable . . .

Tommy is in the kingdom today because he had a mother and grandmother who fasted and prayed for him. He was high on their agenda with God; they were not going to let him go. Now the next generations are the focus of him and his mother. So the legacy rolls on.

Our personal generations are redeemable; your children and

your grandchildren are your seed, water them, nurture them. Don't let go of your generations. The influence expands as the years pass; your heritage is their heritage.

I was in Scotland taking a conference, and noticed an elderly gentleman who kept going in and out. I asked if he was all right and was told that he had planted a forest and had to keep going to check that rabbits, etc., were not eating it and killing all the young shoots. I then asked how long it took to grow a forest and was told about 30 years, but this was for his son so that when his son was older he would have a pension. His father had done the same for him!

I then understood that this was what God was saying to us. Will we sow and toil for something that we will never reap so that the generation after us can see the fruit? They will then do the same for the generation following. In this way every generation's needs will be met.

Dr Margaret Idahosa (from Africa) writes of Daisy Osborne:

> Even though she is not with us today, the seeds that she has sown in Africa – and in my life – will live and keep on producing fruit for ever. The Bible says, 'Tell your children and let your children tell their children, and their children the next generation' (Joel 1:3). I say today, 'Mama Daisy . . . The seed that you sowed in me and in the lives of women and men in Africa will keep producing fruit. We will tell it to our children and our children will tell their children and their children will tell the next generation.'

Dr Idahosa mentions the 'seed that has been left through T. L. and Daisy.' The Bible talks much about seed. It is used in the context of physical seed that reproduces a baby, sometimes it is the word 'descendants', or 'posterity', but it can also be used in the spiritual context. The fruit sown will keep on producing fruit for ever as it is passed on generationally. Dr Idahosa has caught the vision of passing on to the next generation. Africa will always remember their names as lasting memorials.

God has given you the ability to sow lasting seed too. Don't let low self-esteem convince you that you have nothing to sow. God has put in us his life, and his kingdom, everything he gives us is to give away.

As you receive his love: sow it; as you receive his joy: sow it; as you learn to minister: disciple another. You will find what you have to give is in who you are, in your God-given gifts and abilities, in your relationships with God and people. You have more than you ever imagined, lay hold of it, nurturing, protecting and passing it on. This is bigger than your own family, what you have to give your family you can also give others and be spiritual parents to them.

In two generations your legacy can live on in more people than you will touch today.

We may, or may not, be called to be present-day world changers but we are called to be generation changers. There is something in those two testimonies that we can all identify with: a vision to perpetuate and to leave a legacy for the coming generations.

Some of your legacy will pass on without your being proactive, but this will be a mixture of what is redeemed and unredeemed, of good seed and weeds. Lay hold of the redeemed, work on the unredeemed, change the way you live and relate by drawing close to you the younger generations.

Past heritage

I hope the following story will inspire you both to understand and to discover your own heritage:

My granddaughter is 3 years old. She is sixth generation in our family tree. During the process of writing this book I wanted to find out what generation she was in our spiritual family tree.

This is an era when many people are researching their family history and making family trees. I wanted her to have the greatest history of all to pass on – her spiritual roots. So I made enquiries with my own mother. In the course of the conversation she told me that when her grandparents were a young married couple they were spiritualists on the streets of London until they had an encounter with William Booth (founder of the Salvation Army) who led them to Jesus.

Something inside me exploded. I have always had a respect for the Salvation Army; I quote them in my books and when I speak at conferences, and a couple of years ago I read William Booth's life story. I have never had the same strength of feeling about Spurgeon, Wycliffe or other great men of God. William Booth is my hero! Now I discovered why: he is my spiritual ancestor and birthed our spiritual generations.

Then I began to think about the values he held and I related to so many of them. His wife and children were fully involved in all he did; he passed onto them his heritage, sowed seeds into their lives. Every generation was mobilised in the army he built; he sent the people out to the lost. So my discovery enabled me to find out more about myself and to give my children and my children's children this precious gift.

My children, and my grandchildren will be told of this heritage. It will be theirs and each generation will add to it. The Lord is building the house, generation upon generation.

So it is possible to research both physical and spiritual generations, to discover what God has given and search out your heritage. Then you will start to understand and have faith and vision for it to impact your lives. This discovery for me is only a little of what has given me a sense of foundation, and vision to continue to build!

> Those who are among you shall build up the old waste places. You shall raise up the foundations of many generations. (Isaiah 58:12)

We may think that we can't do anything about the generations past, that we should only focus on the generations to come, but here Isaiah is talking about raising those foundations up, the foundations of generations that have gone before. We can build on the foundations of the previous generations. Preceding generations are our heritage, just as we are building for the future, so our ancestors built for us.

Those foundations can be discovered, if we will take the time to look for them. Foundations are hidden. When an archaeologist wants to discover the past he will dig deep but he will dig carefully so that among the dirt and dust he can find the treasure. What is in your heritage, the heritage of your city, or your nation that you can build on? We have a cathedral in the city where I live, and I find it a tremendous privilege to praise God in that place. I recognise the heritage of the generations of saints who have praised God in that place. I attend events where Christians in the area come together to worship God in a style so different from the saints of old, yet the liberty that we have in worship is built on those foundations.

As I share this with others their past starts to come to life. If your past is one which has no Christian foundations, it still has a heritage for you in it. All good things belong to God, so in your inheritance, there are good things that you can inherit from generations past. Look for the godly values that were in those generations. For example, you can have generations before you who did not know God, or serve him, but you see how they treated their children with honour, and the best they knew how. I believe that within those values was an anointing that could have come forth with great power had they been given over to God. Those anointings could be waiting for you!

God gives gifts; if the enemy has stolen and abused them, they are still in your generational line to redeem. Activate, walk in and have faith for the blessing. Don't just walk under the curse, receive your inheritance and propel it into the generations to come.

> Because he loved your forefathers and chose their descendants after them, he brought you out of Egypt by his Presence and his great strength, to drive out before you nations greater and stronger than you and to bring you into their land to give it to you for your inheritance. (Deuteronomy 4:37-38)

In this Scripture God is again affirming the destiny of the generations, affirming his love and commitment to the past and to those that would follow. They were chosen by him, they were not by chance. Our ancestors were loved, we are chosen. He was working out his plans through them to establish them in the land that he had promised Abraham. Each generation being part of that final purpose. One generation was promised the land, another fled captivity and saw the promise, and another took residence. Each generation understanding the heritage promised to their forefathers and walking in faith to see its fulfilment.

In Acts 3:25 Peter continues to remind 'all the people' (men women, young people and children) of their heritage: 'You are heirs of the prophets and of the covenant God made with your fathers.'

This is our heritage, our birthright. We are heirs of the prophets; how much better than any earthly succession, and the covenant of God is our legal inherited right. He is looking today for prophets who will remind us of his covenants and restore again the command to pass them on to our children (Psalm 78:1-8). To pass on in word and deed just like his servant David, who was a living epistle to his children and his generation.

I spoke to a couple in San Francisco who were Messianic Jews and they told me how they had lost their roots when the Temple fell and the Greek culture moved in. They were in the process of digging deep into their heritage in order that they could grow from it. Their heritage is our heritage too, because of the grace and mercy of God to us, and from these roots God has continued to grow the generations.

Future heritage

> David said, 'So now I charge you in the sight of all Israel [men, women, young people and children] and of the assembly of the Lord, and in the hearing of our God: Be careful to follow all the commands of the Lord your God, that you may possess this good land and pass it on as an inheritance to your descendants for ever. And you, my son Solomon, acknowledge the God of your father, and serve him with whole-hearted devotion and with a willing mind.' (1 Chronicles 28:8-9)

David was speaking to every generation, making special mention of his son, charging them to be obedient to the Most High God, so that they would not only live in the land, but also hold themselves accountable to their descendants. They were entrusted with the land for their own generation and also for those who would come after them.

Whatever we are given, we are given in trust for future generations. Consider how much care is taken with property such as houses, land, jewellery and works of art which are promised to future generations, yet our spiritual heritage, which is of eternal value, is underrated as a legacy. Don't let's be careless, or short-sighted. Take stock of what you have and begin to see how you can pass this on to future generations. Make a spiritual will!

I find it interesting that in the story of the prodigal son the father, depicted as a good father, gave his sons their inheritance when he was asked for it. This father would have known the strength and weaknesses of both sons, yet he gave to both unconditionally. His heart was, above all, for them to have their heritage. That is the heart of God, for us to have all that is ours, and our spiritual heritage is freely given. We can squander, ignore and abuse it or we can treasure what is ours and pass it on to our children.

Many do not look to pro-actively pass on to the next generation because they have no focus to do so; their belief in their own self-worth is so low that they do not consider themselves worthy of perpetuating something of themselves into the coming generations. This is a lie that perpetuates the enemy's devices to rob future generations.

Everything God gives is for our generation and the generations to come. The church today would be so much more powerful if it had understood this. We would be living in such a heritage, a heritage of thousands of years. If the people of Israel had seen the land just for their generation their attitude to it would have been totally different.

We must see that we are custodians of what God has done and is doing in our nations, churches, and lives today. This is the heritage of future generations. Strength and beauty will come as we activate the past, live in it, add our own contribution and propel it into the future.

When God blesses you today it is for your physical and spiritual children and your children's children after you. We are to treasure the work of God in our lives, the prophetic words and the blessings he gives us 'that [we] may possess the good land and pass it on as an inheritance to [our] descendants for ever'.

How we live in holiness and obedience before God will protect the territory given to us.

Covenant heritage

I will establish my covenant as an everlasting covenant between me and you and your descendants after you for the generations to come, to be your God and the God of your descendants after you. The whole land of Canaan, where you are now an alien, I will give as an everlasting possession to you and your descendants after you; and I will be their God. (Genesis 17:7-8)

And so it was remembered with Moses, when God identified himself as the God of three generations and said:

Go up to the land I promised on oath to Abraham, Isaac and Jacob, saying I will give it to your descendants. (Exodus 33:1)

None of this happened 'by chance'. God chose Abraham because he knew Abraham would pass on what God had given him to his children and would establish and model that for the future generation (Genesis 18:19).

He also knew that Abraham understood God's heart for his children. Genesis 22 tells how Abraham was prepared to sacrifice this son of promise because of his complete devotion to the living God. It was then that God gave him the nations because he had understood the Father heart of God who one day would sacrifice his own son.

God told him, 'I will make your descendants as numerous as the stars in the sky and I will give them all these lands, and through your offspring all nations on earth will be blessed.' (Genesis 26:4)

This covenant could only be fulfilled if he had a son to continue his generational line.

The device of the enemy was to try and rob Abraham of his natural offspring, so that the promises of God could not be fulfilled.

Today there are many barren couples that long for a child. I believe this God-given desire for children is not just about fulfilling the fathering and mothering desires. It is a heart cry for future generations that will come to birth through the longed-for child. It is a cry from the heart of God. As the living expression of our Father we need to destroy the works of the evil one who seeks to rob the furtherance of the generations. A barren couple means the end of the generational line of their particular family. The only end of the generational line is God himself . . . it is his role!

Similarly abortion destroys not just a child, but also the forthcoming generations of that child's seed.

As we begin to understand generational blessing and heritage so we will be able to rise up more effectively.

> I have made a covenant with my chosen one, I have sworn to David my servant, 'I will establish your line for ever and make your throne firm through all generations.' (Psalm 89:3-4)

David's descendants had this promise; you have promises that you can live in, and these are for you and for your children and for your children's children. Tell them, live them and pass them on. When these promises are alive within us then they will cause faith to rise and the fulfilment to be seen. I see people investigating the curses in their family in order to break them, and this is good, but when we begin to see the blessing and walk in that, the curses will go quicker, and find no room to return.

Spend some time considering the promises that God has given. Look back through the generations, ask questions about your family, trust God to bring them to light, then, in discovering them remember them, talk about them and look for them to be fulfilled in your generations, speak them into the generations to come.

Let's lift our faith to restore generational promises. God needs the ears of the church to be open to hear him and to be faithful custodians.

I remember a young couple telling me about the birth of their tiny son. They attended a church where someone told them about a prophecy given to that church many years ago. It said that no one from that church would lose a child conceived in the womb. After they had conceived the wife became very ill and the hospital told her that her womb could no longer carry the baby. Then they remembered the promise, and although it had been given many, many years before, they believed and would not allow surgery.

As they told me I looked into the eyes of the little baby I was holding and knew he was a child of that promise.

Passing it on!

Memorials to remember!

God told the people of Israel many times to build memorials, and to have feasts for two reasons. That they would remember what God had done, and that they would have reminders for their children and their descendants. He gave them strategies to ensure the blessing would be remembered and that the stories would be passed on. Our Creator knows us best and knows that these are effective methods for securing the present into the future.

He knows our frailty – that we forget the wonderful things he has done for us and that we might not pass on to the next generation, and so he has given us ways that will help us. As we start to restore this momentous blessing, we need to restore the tangible evidence that we were given to help us.

The memorial of Passover or Lord's Supper

This is one of the times of remembrance that God gave his people to establish a testimony for generations past and generations to come.

Vision

Exodus gives the account of the way God rescued his people from the land of Egypt. Pharaoh repeatedly refused to let the children of Israel go.

God told Moses to tell Pharaoh, 'By now I could have stretched out my hand and struck you and your people . . . But I have raised you up for this very purpose that I might show you my power and that my name might be proclaimed in all the earth.' (Exodus 9:15-16)

Here was God's vision: 'that my name might be proclaimed in all the earth.'

System

Then in Exodus 10:1-2 God said to Moses:

I have hardened his heart and the hearts of his officials so that I may perform these miraculous signs of mine among them that you may tell your children and grand-children how I dealt harshly with the Egyptians and how I performed my signs among them, and that you may know that I am the Lord.

This was the system that God would use to spread his name in all the earth. His miraculous signs were to be told to the children, and their grandchildren. One generation passing the story of God's deliverance to the other.

Method

In Exodus 12: 2, 3, 14, 24 the Israelites were given a method to ensure this would be accomplished. Moses told the people how to celebrate the Passover:

Tell the whole Israelite community [men, women, young people and children] that on the tenth day of this month each man is to take a lamb for his family . . . If any household is too small for a lamb they must share with their nearest neighbour . . . This is the day you are to commemorate; for the generations to come you shall celebrate it as a festival to the Lord – a lasting ordinance.

Obey these instructions as a lasting ordinance for you and your descendants.

The name of God was to be taken to the nations, as one generation told the next in a feast to be celebrated in the homes. So important was it that he even gave space for the children to interact and be fully involved (12:26) so they would clearly understand what their God had done.

By following these instructions the people of Israel would pass on the miraculous signs from generation to generation.

Vision affirmed

Jesus affirmed the vision which today is unchanged: that the great commission is to be fulfilled and the Gospel taken to every nation . . . Then the time came for Jesus to celebrate the Passover with his disciples. Jesus affirmed this time of remembrance, and exploded every concept of deliverance as he, the Lamb of God, was on the eve of taking away the sin of the world and setting every captive free (Luke 22).

Method continued

> After his death 'they continued to meet together in the temple courts. They broke bread in their homes and ate together with glad and sincere hearts, praising God and enjoying favour with all the people. And the Lord added to their number daily those who were being saved.' (Acts 2:42-47)

As the early church was being birthed they remembered the Lamb of God, the Passover Lamb, as they celebrated in their homes. Could it be that today we have lost this simple act of remembrance from our homes. In this relational, interactive environment the life and the impartation of the salvation of God for his people is remembered.

Acts of remembrance that carry on generationally are most

profound in the home, as with Christmas and Thanksgiving. Each nation has its traditions when the family comes together. Even governments recognise this and declare public holidays.

Generally we have abdicated the Lord's Supper to be the responsibility of the Church. There is nothing wrong with us celebrating it corporately but we need to restore it to our homes. If our households are too small join with others, as God commanded the people of Israel, so that in the relational intimacy of the home we remember to pass on the memory of the greatest sign and wonder in all history, and at the same time recount our own salvation experience. His miraculous signs commemorated for the generations to come, one generation telling the other!

My personal strategies include always having children and young people in my life. They are first my friends but they travel with me, and serve with me. As I talk with them, as they watch my life, so I believe they will receive and be custodians of what God has imparted to me. I write materials so that the vision can be read:

> Let this be recorded for the generation yet unborn, a people yet to be created shall praise the Lord. (Psalm 102:18)

David wrote for future generations. The psalms are still used.

'Keep it so they can see'

In Exodus 16:32 Moses said,

> 'This is what the Lord commanded: "Take a jar of manna and keep it for the generations to come, so they can see the bread I gave you to eat in the desert when I brought you out of Egypt."'

When God provides miraculously for us, how do we make sure we remember? My daughter was very sick during her early years and our faithful God healed her. So we have kept some of the medical equipment that she needed during the early years and from time to time we look at it, or she shows someone as she recounts her story of the faithfulness of God to her.

Her medical equipment is a memorial, just as the jar of manna was for the children of Israel.

In Joshua 3 the story of the separation of the Jordan is related and then in chapter 4:5-7 it goes on to say:

> Each of you is to take up a stone on his shoulder, according to the number of the tribes of Israel, to serve as a sign among you. In the future when your children ask you, 'What do these stones mean?' Tell them . . . 'These stones are to be a memorial to the people of Israel for ever.'

The stone memorial was for two reasons:

First, 'To serve as a sign among you.' They were for the generation living at that time, establishing a sign of the miracle-working power of their God. They were a reminder to them of the hand of God working on their behalf.

Second, as a means of provoking their children to ask questions so that they too were reminded of how great and mighty their God was. So the story would be established on earth and passed from generation to generation.

God knows how to establish his testimony firmly within the generations. We can restore memorials, so they not only remind us of what God has done but also provide tangible evidence and reminders for coming generations. They become heritages to be passed on.

For example: when God has delivered you financially take some paper money, frame it and put on the wall. Then you will remember that your God is your Jehovah Jireh, and when the children ask why there is money in a picture frame you will tell them!

When your children prayed and were healed make a memorial that will remind them of the miracle-working power of their God.

You may end up with a home that looks different from the one you have today but you will have a story to tell everyone who asks. Your children will know the stories and remember that the hand of the Lord is powerful and so always fear the Lord.

Deuteronomy 6:8-9,12 commands us to have visual reminders for ourselves and our children:

> Tie them as symbols on your hands and bind them on your foreheads. Write them on the door-frames of your houses and on your gates . . .be careful that you do not forget the Lord who brought you out of Egypt.

This is being restored today as people wear WWJD (What Would Jesus Do?) bracelets; cars have the symbol of the fish and nameplates on the doors of houses are declarations about that home.

My friends have a fireplace where you would expect to see costly or beautiful ornaments on display. As you enter their sitting room you see a display that seems to make no sense from a decorative point of view. Each object displayed is a memorial – a lighthouse to remind them of the goodness of God in providing our church centre called 'the Lighthouse Centre', a hand-painted egg given as a 50th wedding anniversary gift to Tony's father, so reminding them of their godly heritage in marriage, a medal reminding them of a prophetic word where the medal was mentioned and so on.

I remember these because I have heard them explained to so many people, and each time that they explain, my friends are reminded of the faithfulness of their God.

The Temple was built with symbolism to be a lasting memorial of the Almighty God in the place where they worshipped and sacrificed. Nehemiah challenged Sanballat because of his lack of memorials in Jerusalem. For Nehemiah they were a sign of their heritage and ownership of the city!

On one occasion Samuel was sacrificing to the Lord and the Philistines tried to engage the Israelites in battle. At that very moment, 'the Lord thundered with a loud thunder against the Philistines' (1 Samuel 7:10) and they were thrown into panic. Samuel's reaction was to set up a stone and name it Ebenezer. 'Thus far has the Lord helped us.'

When God thunders from heaven on your behalf, or on behalf of your family or church 'set up a stone', raise a memorial!

David wrote in Psalm 102:18, 'Let this be written for a future generation, that a people not yet created may praise you.'

The written word is a remembrance to future generations. How many of us have written down for our future generations those things that we want them to remember? This book is written so that the vision will be before the eyes of generations yet to come. The habit of writing diaries has faded from our cultures as we rush from one day to the next, and so the memories fade as the memorial is abandoned.

God knows our frailty, that we forget and our children and the generations to come miss out, so he has given us the way to establish his testimony on earth . . . memorials!

We have the risen lamb of God who made the final sacrifice, so let's make creative memorials, not so they can be worshipped but so they are literally what the Bible says they should be: reminders to us and to our children and their children after them! They will be a witness and a heritage for the generations to come. They will become precious treasures to future generations who are still telling the story!

Let's restore to our churches, homes and our communities memorials as an everlasting memory.

From hiddenness to holiness

The environment plays a large part in the health of anything that lives and grows. Similarly the environment in which our children and young people grow will have a significant effect on them. They need pure air in which to breathe, they need a pure environment in their homes and among the community of Christ to grow healthily in body, soul and spirit.

As we take responsibility and 'clean up' the environment by our repentance, the result must be the next generation developing with greater purity and health.

My hope is that by bringing to light those things that have remained hidden, we can walk away from them. By remaining hidden they prevent the flow of the blessing to the youngest generation.

The most 'hidden' command

I believe that one of the most hidden commands in the Bible is that we should tell our children, the next generation, of the miracle-working, sign-giving, faithful, powerful God we are called to serve. This command is repeated many times in Scripture. It is a command that is rarely preached, and little demand placed on obedience to it.

Children love to hear our stories, to hear those things that are important to us. We tell them about our favourite soccer teams, our choice in music, and our favourite food. But so often children do not know the testimonies of the previous generation as told to them from their parents and those around them. We have become so peer orientated that our first thought is to tell our own age group. I have been in situations where parents have given a testimony in a small group and their own children have never heard it.

We need to restore the heritage of telling our children before we tell those outside our family. Those who have no birth children are still commanded 'to tell the next generation the wonderful works of God, his power to all who are to come'.

Moses' last command to the children of Israel is:

> Take to heart all the words that I have spoken to you today, so that you may command your children to obey carefully all the words of the law. (Deuteronomy 32:46)

The first part of fulfilling the command effectively is to take the words of God into our hearts. Words and commands given from the heart are very different. They are given with enthusiasm, with personal connection and faith, they become part of us.

Today the word 'command' is disliked and avoided. We like to persuade, to convince, and to allow for freedom of choice. These attributes are excellent in the right context, but when the Almighty God uses the word 'command' we have no right to dilute or change his meaning.

His command to us is to pass on to our children and the next generation, with the Father's heart of unconditional love, yet with a clear commission. In the same way the children are to obey him as they see his reflection in us.

Psalm 78:1-4 is a key passage:

> Give ear, oh my people to my law. Incline your ears to the words of my mouth. I will open my mouth in a parable. I will utter dark sayings of old, which we have heard and known and our fathers have told us. We will not hide them from our children, we will tell the next generation.

These verses speak of 'hiding them from our children'. 'Hiding' is a pro-active word. The Bible does not allow for passive ignorance. When we keep quiet, things are hidden from the next generation. Maoris in Australia take time to recount their stories, they keep them alive in their own hearts and the hearts of the generations coming after them. Their heritage is secure as long as they remember to do this. So important is it to them that they have rituals for doing it.

Telling to the generation to come the praises of God and his wonderful works he has done. (Psalm 78:4)

My prayer is that you get excited about the impact that you can have. Your stories can live long on the earth. I love going out with children or young people and telling them the stories of my travels, the miracles, and the funny moments. They get excited and become involved. I was ill on one trip and received an email saying that a child from the small group I belonged to had prayed that I would receive a bunch of flowers. As I read that email there came a knock on the door. There stood a gentleman with a bunch of flowers for me. That child had heard of the praise of God and the wonderful works he has done . . . I will keep that story alive for her for the rest of her childhood, and while I do so it will stay alive for me!

For he established a testimony in Jacob, and appointed a law in Israel commanding our fathers that they should make them known to their children. (Psalm 78:5; Amplified Bible)

This is a command of the Almighty God. It is not an option in our lives. It is the way God made us to be secure in our heritage. Laws were given to Israel: life has been given to us. The Holy Spirit has taken up residence with us, and we are sons and daughters of the living God. We must make this known to our children. This is the throne of God being established on the earth, it is his dominion being protected and the next generation's future being secured.

As I travel I see many things that are the same from nation to nation. One of these is that everyone wants a better future for their children. This will not come by the Body of Christ abdicating its responsibility to that generation. Our children's future is in the hands of each one of us.

> That the generation to come might know them, the children who will be born. (Psalm 78:6)

We have through our obedience the ability to impact generations that will come after us. God trusts us with them; he has made us responsible for them. We are able to impact the generations as yet unborn, and bring the glory of God to welcome the unborn.

> If you pay attention to these laws and are careful to follow them, then the Lord your God will keep his covenant of love with you . . . He will bless the fruit of your womb . . . (Deuteronomy 7:12-13)

> If you carefully follow the commands I give you today, the Lord your God will set you high above all the nations of the earth. All these blessings will come upon you . . . the fruit of your womb will be blessed if you fully obey the Lord your God. (Deuteronomy 28:1, 4)

Our walk with God can secure the future of those as yet unborn. What a vision, to reach beyond those generations that are on the earth with us and begin to secure the heritage of the unborn.

> That they may arise and declare them to their children. (Psalm 78:6)

If we re-establish this generational flow, it will be far easier for our children to continue it, for they will have seen us (modelling), and, recognising the place we held in their lives, make it a priority for their children. We live our lives the way that we were brought up as children. It may be that you never had that modelling yourself, but one generation has to rise up and break the cycle for the sake of the next.

Then they may set their hope in God and not forget the works of God but keep his commandments. (Psalm 78:7)

In some scriptures it says, 'In this way, they would set their hope in God.' In what way? When you tell it to your children.

This verse is the pivotal one in this Psalm. 'THEN they will set their hope in God, not forget his commandments and always obey what he has done.'

A survey in New Zealand showed that 80 per cent of children brought up in Christian families were not taking their place in Church. In America, a survey was done of churched and unchurched students. They questioned them on morality, honesty, drugs, sexuality and other such issues. There was no difference between the two results. There were as many honest unchurched and as many immoral churched. Something has gone wrong. We've had good children's ministry and thank God for it, that's a part of what God has given us, but there's been a whole part missing: the generational flow. In his perfect time and his perfect season, he is now bringing it to light.

The Father has been building from generation, to generation; this is your generation. He is restoring to us the commands that have passed us by unnoticed. 'He commanded our forefathers to teach their children, SO the next generation would know them, even the children yet to be born, and they in turn would tell their children. THEN they would put their trust in God.'

'THEN' is when we pass on generationally and secure their 'hope in God' so they 'will not forget his commands and always obey what he has done'. What greater incentive could we need that that?

There is no age limit to this; he doesn't say that there is an age when we stop telling our children. Each society sets ages for adulthood and releases parents and the other generations from their responsibilities. I have heard people preach, with their children listening to the lesson, 'When they are 18, they'll have to leave home,' and the children hearing this were at that time 4 years old. We are too quick to see ourselves 'released' from our generational responsibilities.

He has commanded us to tell our children.

The most 'hidden' prayer

> Oh Lord, from my youth I have known you. Even now, when I'm old and grey, don't let me die until I have told the next generation the wonderful works of God, your power to all who is to come. (Psalm 71:17-18)

Sometimes I have the tremendous privilege of speaking to the oldest generation. I always use this verse as my springboard and challenge them by asking how often they pray this prayer of David, how often they rend the heavens asking to stay on this earth long enough to tell the next generation, realising that they have the power to change the destiny not only of the generations on the earth but those as yet unborn.

Let it be on our lips until the day we walk into eternity: 'Oh God, don't let me die until I have told the next generation the wonderful works of God.'

I challenge them with the commitment of Eli who took in a child, even though his own had left home and gone astray. Each time some of them come to me with tears in their eyes and thank me, saying that they have been told that they should be respected, that they should be honoured but that no one has challenged them and given them a purpose to be on the earth and impact the kingdom in such a major way.

Those who have known Jesus from youth are a storehouse of treasure holding our inheritance. God forgive us that we do not take the time to receive what is ours and release that treasure from the burial of years.

The most 'hidden' testimony

'Oh Lord, from my youth I have known you.' (Psalm 71:17)

David's declaration at the beginning of this verse can be overlooked in the same way that this testimony is overlooked in the Church today.

The testimony is, 'I was born into a Christian family, my parents discipled me, through my teenage years I stayed true to God, I have married a believer and I am discipling my children.'

This is the testimony of all testimonies. It is the testimony of normal Christian growth. It is the testimony of the saving, keeping power of the Lord Jesus Christ.

I would like to see this testimony exposed and given the honour it so rightly deserves.

I have teenagers say to me, 'I haven't got a testimony, because I haven't gone into drugs and fallen away from God.' We need to restore heroes of the faith for them to honour and aspire to, men and women who have stayed faithful to their God and who are a testimony to their faithful parents.

Let's honour these people, some of them may be really old, some of them young parents, some single people who have chosen to stay unmarried rather than marry and be 'unequally yoked'.

Let's bring back that testimony to our pulpits, in our small groups, in our conversations and shout it from the rooftops: 'Oh God, from my youth you have taught me. And to this day, to this day, even if I am old and grey, I declare your wondrous works.'

What a testimony!

The most 'avoided' sin

Read Matthew 18:1-14 before you read on any further, because I have met very few people who have read these 14 verses in context.

I want to challenge the heart of every believer. The whole passage is networked to bring the Body of Christ into holiness. This chapter may seem as if it is focused on children, but as you look at it closely I believe the focus for Jesus is the heart of every believer. It is about bringing us into a greater degree of holiness.

'At that time, the disciples came to Jesus saying, "Who then is the greatest in the kingdom of heaven?" [And then Jesus] called a little child and had him stand among them'; and in Mark 9:36 it says that he took the child in his arms.

Children loved Jesus, no child would be held by someone with whom they felt unsafe, or insecure. Children go to happy, caring fun people! They must have been around Jesus, because he did not have to go and find a child when asked the question, the child was right there with him already.

So Jesus put the child right among them. In Mark 10:13 we read how he rebuked the disciples for preventing the people from bringing the children to him. Jesus wanted the children right where he was.

Children have the God-given right to be where the presence of Jesus is. Jesus was making it very clear to the disciples that the children are to have an unhindered path to his presence. Even those considering themselves his closest friends were to maintain access for the children. What implications does this have for the rest of the Body of Christ?

Jesus didn't place conditions on the state of the children who were welcome: the rich and the poor, those in the streets and those in the palaces, those who are dirty and those who are in the latest fashions, those who are sick and those who are our finest athletes, those who live among the garbage and those who have homes where they are loved and accepted. All have the right to come to the presence of Jesus and the older generations are to 'forbid them not'. Where Jesus is they are very welcome, where the anointing is they have God-given right to be.

> And Jesus called a little child and set him in the midst of them and said, 'Assuredly, I say to you, unless you are converted and become as little children, you will by no means enter the kingdom of heaven. Therefore, whoever humbles himself as this little child is greatest in the kingdom of heaven.' (Matthew 18:2-3)

In coming to Jesus we are to come as little children. This does not mean childishly but rather childlikeness, and there's a whole difference between those two. Children come with uncluttered faith, expecting to be loved unconditionally with every need met.

> Whoever humbles himself as this little child is greatest in the kingdom of heaven. (Matthew 18:4)

Children are as much our role models as we are theirs. If we don't have any children in our lives, how do we know how to be great in the kingdom of heaven? We all walk away from our childhood and our memories grow dim as we become so-called sophisticated adults. We have forgotten what it is to come as little children. It is a privilege to have them in our lives. If someone came to you and asked how to be great in the kingdom of heaven, would YOU show them a child?

That is the Word of God. Who do we receive when we receive a child? Jesus. If we don't receive a child, who don't we receive? If we insult a child, who do we insult? If we belittle a child, who do we belittle? If we despise a child, whom do we despise? If we exalt a child and encourage, whom do we exalt and encourage? Jesus.

We need to constantly remind ourselves of this. Many of

you will have read that scripture many times but have you really understood its impact? We need to be awesomely aware that in the face of our children is the face of the Lord Jesus Christ; then our hearts will change, our relationship with them will change and, not only that, our relationship with Jesus will change.

Jesus says, 'As you receive them, so you receive me.' These words are not spoken to a specific group of people, they are spoken to everyone. Many times I remember these words when I need to correct my attitude to a 'little one' and it always corrects my heart.

> But whoever causes one of these little ones who believe in me to sin, it will be better for him if a millstone were hung round his neck and he were drowned in the depths of the sea. (Matthew 18:5-6)

Jesus says, 'If you're going to sin in this area, go and kill yourself.' This is the only sin that he speaks about in this way. A millstone is BIG!

Jesus knew the vulnerability of children and the impact other generations could make on their lives. When older generations hinder a child they have the potential to hinder that child through teenage years and into adulthood. A damaged adult can bring up damaged children and so the generations that follow can all be affected by damaging a child.

Satan is well aware of this, and evidence of his destruction on the lives of children is all around us. In every nation he is seeking to destroy childhood, and even to abort their entry into the world.

God gave the older generations responsibility for them, to nurture, protect and reveal his glory to them. We are the custodians of their generation.

How is it that this sin is so avoided in the Church today? I have never heard it preached with an altar call for those who wish to repent of it. I have never heard of people having ministry because of a wrong attitude to children, we pass it by, we avoid it.

Think of the things that cause you to stumble . . . being ignored, being spoken to inappropriately, not being listened to, not being recognised, included and understood. These things cause children to stumble too.

If I am walking up the street or if people come into church, I always make sure I speak to the children first. If you are walking up the street, and you've got children with you, I will always stop and speak to the children first, because I do not want to ignore the face of Jesus. If we start interacting adult to adult, the children run off and we loose the moment to welcome them. We must not be a stumbling block to them.

If you knew somebody who was committing adultery, you might make it a matter of prayer. If you knew a fellow Christian who was stealing from the offering, somebody would be taking some action. If you had a Christian friend who had a habit of lying then you might look for them to receive ministry. But how often do you minister to people who have a problem in their attitude to children? How often do people come forward and say, 'I need help. I've got a problem in my attitude to children?' How often do we hear people weep and cry before God, 'God change me, I need your heart for your little ones'?

It is a sin we avoid confronting and have learned to live with.

As an awareness of the seriousness of this sin comes upon us, let's bring a spirit of repentance to people (just as we would with other sins) and so bring restoration and holiness to the Body of Christ.

God says, 'Be ye holy as I am holy.' Repentance must come to the people of God and the cry, 'Create in me a clean heart.' Jesus is preparing the bride!

'If your hand or your foot causes you to sin, then it would

be better for you to be lame or maimed than to do that. And if your eye causes you to sin, pluck it out.' (Matthew 18:8-9) We know the sort of sins that are raged against children in terms of abuse. Lots of them start with the eye. We know the cruelty that is raged against children; lots of it starts with the hand and the feet. There is no mistaking the awesome severity of the Lord Jesus Christ in relation to these things.

> Take heed that you do not despise one of these little ones. For I tell you that their angels in heaven always see the face of my Father in heaven. (Matthew 18:10)

Despise means: 'Look down on'. How easy it is to fall into that attitude. Jesus immediately elevates the children right into the throne room of God. He has representatives of the children, angels, who look right into the face of their heavenly Father on their behalf. Not one child is missed.

Jesus tells the story of the 100 sheep and the one that goes missing, finishing with 'Even so, it is not the will of your Father who is in heaven that one of these little ones should perish' (verse 14).

Have you ever noticed that the story of the 100 sheep is about children in this Gospel? He will go after the one child and leave the 99.

Have you ever heard it said, 'They are only a children'? How quick are we to meet the needs of the adults, to ensure that they have the best. Jesus requires that we re-examine our priorities. Go after a child who is lost, for they can't find their own way back.

If a child goes missing from home, an operation is put in place to find them. It becomes priority and no one rests until they are found. So it must be with the children who are lost to Jesus. High priority and no rest until they are found, every available person mobilised . . . a full-scale operation with Jesus heading the search party!

Let these 14 verses be a challenge to us every day of our lives.

Let's look at two other things that will attack the healthy flow through the generations:

First, the 'spirit of abortion'. How many times have Christians said things like, 'I haven't really got time to have children in my life', 'I can't do things the way I want if children are around', 'I didn't plan to have them like this', 'It would be far too costly if I actually accommodate some children in my life'.

These statements are often spoken in the context of the life of the Church, but they are the very words that are often spoken in the doctor's surgery by someone who is asking for an abortion.

When the church rises up on behalf of the children in thought, word and deed then we will have greater strength to defy the power of evil in the world around us.

Speak life to this generation, welcome them, nurture them, lay down your life for them and bring them from birth to maturity. Or we will be party to the thwarting of the plans and purposes of God for this generation of children.

Second, the 'spirit of rebellion'. How many times have you said of a teenager, 'Oh, well, of course, they're just going through the teenage rebellious period'? 'Teenagers are so disobedient', 'Wait until they are teenagers, then you won't have a good relationship with them'. I don't hear many people saying, 'Adults are so noisy', etc. We would be really affronted if this were the case. Yet these things are said of the teenagers and children.

When we say, in word or deed, to our children, 'It will be boring for you being with us', or ' We don't want you around because we don't want to adapt to your culture', then we shouldn't wonder why they leave us and don't have any vision for being Church as they become young adults.

Normality in the kingdom is having teenagers that stay in relationship with other generations, and remain on fire for

God. This is the way that God planned it, and this is what he wants to restore. Don't make plans for estrangement and rebellion, make plans for unity. Let one generation bless the other in word and deed.

Normality is health and wholeness, which aligns with the Word of God and kingdom culture.

Generational anointing

Anointing can be passed on from generation to generation. The anointing on William Booth, the founder of the Salvation Army, has been passed on from generation to generation both physically and spiritually. He recognised the call on his life and the destiny of his children to make a difference. His generations are still walking in that anointing because he brought his children right into the vision and made it their vision too. He and his wife Catherine were passionate about the call of God and his children caught it.

They saw what God was doing and loved it enough to want to claim it as their descendants' destiny too.

William Booth came home one day and said that he had seen people sleeping under London Bridge. His son commented that he knew they were there, and had already seen them.

At that point William Booth asked him how long ago it was that he first noticed them.

'Oh,' he said, 'about two years ago.'

To which William Booth replied, 'Then why have you done nothing about it?'

He brought the next generation right in to where the anointing could be passed on. Whatever God gives us is to be passed on. He trusts us with that legacy. Similarly there are anointings in our past that are waiting for us to receive them. A mighty dam, waiting to burst through, even to a thousand generations.

Passing on the anointing

The precious anointing of an Almighty, Holy God is awesome. I want us to consider how this affects our children and how we can either defile or present a holy anointing to them.

God has entrusted us with visions, gifts, and passion. His trust is that we use them to his glory and multiply them through discipleship. They are the heritage of the younger generation. Don't deny them that heritage; let it be your greatest joy to relationally pass it on to them.

I was recently in a church in the USA and they encourage everyone in leadership to disciple one of the younger generation. Two young teenagers, overseen by a man, were operating the tape and video recording. The drummer in the worship band had a young lad watching him during the praise and worship, and occasionally I saw the drummer get up and let the boy 'have a go'. It seemed as if everyone was being shadowed by the younger generation! What a joy to see the simplicity of the generational heritage of anointing and gifts flowing.

I have repeatedly heard people say, with resignation in their voices, 'He was a pastor's child and that is why he is no longer following Jesus', or, 'They are leaders in a Church, so their children grew up to resent it'. Articles are written in magazines about the problem. It is almost as if we have grown to expect a problem because of a responsibility, vision and anointing.

Who gave that vision? Who gave that calling? Who anointed those parents? God did! If we look at those two statements together, we are saying, 'God, you gave this gift to parents and the end result is that their children's lives are wrecked.'

God is serious about children. He gets angry with those who will harm children or even hinder them. Would God give any parent anything that is going to ruin their children? God's not a liar. He doesn't work against himself.

He only gives parents anointing and ministry that will bless, encourage and result in their children falling deeper in love with Jesus. So, anything that God gives you, any gift, any calling, any ministry, he has given you in order that it blesses your children and every child who touches your life.

The responsibility that is given in carrying that anointing is to bless the next generation with it, just as Paul did with Timothy and Eli with Samuel. God trusts us with his anointing so that we can pass it on to the next generation. The next generation will go further than you. What greater incentive could we need than that. What God has entrusted to me will not die; it will be multiplied from generation to generation, my children and their descendants, my spiritual children and their children. It will be multiplied and each time it will increase.

How do they see it?

So what goes wrong? We must assume responsibility for the way we use that gift.

If you give me a sharp knife I can cut slices of birthday cake for my children, I can carve meat, I can bless my children with this lovely, sharp knife. That knife is sharp and powerful. It is like a two-edged sword. The anointing too is sharp and powerful and sharper than a two-edged sword. It means we need to carry it with a sense of awe and responsibility.

If God had given someone a gift of healing and all the time he was visiting others and praying for them, and because God was using him mightily people came to his home to be prayed for, we might think this was evidence of a servant heart and that he was using the anointing to the full. This may be so, but where are his children, what is their view of a healing ministry?

Their perception is that it takes their father away from them; it causes them pain, it appears to be more loved by their father than they are, and leaves them feeling abandoned. This is an abomination to God.

I knew a worship leader whose husband was an itinerant preacher. She had a two-year-old daughter who sat with somebody else while her mummy led the worship. Frequently she was taken out crying, 'Mummy, Mummy.' One day I stopped and said, 'What is this child learning about worship? What does worship mean to this two-year-old?' It means it's a place of desperate pain, where I'm removed from my Mummy, and where I go through such agony while everybody else is worshipping God. We took measures to address that so that she was with her mother in the ministry God has entrusted to her. This child loves to be in worship now.

Ask yourself, 'What is happening to my children, or other children as a result of what God has given me? What view of ministry am I giving them?'

They need to know that you are there for them and that they are involved. Start looking at what God has given you from their perspective.

We need to repent that we have put condemnation on the precious anointing of God, instead of taking personal responsibility to raise a generation who are excited about the call on their lives, gaining vision and experience as they grow to be like their heroes who made space for them in their walk with God.

They *are* your ministry

When somebody comes and asks, 'I want to know what my ministry is. I have not discovered it yet.' I ask them one question first: 'Have you got children?' If they say yes I always respond, 'Then they are your ministry.'

Before you ask for any other ministry check whether you are bringing up your children to know the Lord Jesus Christ and making disciples of them. Are you giving your children everything you want to give everybody else? If your children are not receiving the best you can give then anything else you do will be built on a shaky foundation.

Imagine you come to my home and I feed you with the

very best that I could offer. I have a tremendous ministry of hospitality. Then my children appear and you see them thin and emaciated, having not eaten for months. You would be shocked and appalled that I was feeding others and leaving my children to starve.

Sadly this is what happens in many ministries. Adults are so busy 'feeding' others and their own children are not receiving that 'food'.

The most important ministry you will ever be given by God, is to disciple your children. I believe if you get that foundation right, every other ministry will just spring to life in an amazing way.

In future, if you are in a position of training and releasing others or if people seek your counsel, lay deep foundations, and raise others who will raise up the next generation.

> They ministered before the tabernacle of the tent with singing . . . performing their service in due order.
> These and their sons served. (1 Chronicles 6:32-33)

> These men [whose grandfathers] David and Samuel had established them to their office of trust. So they and their sons had oversight of the house of the Lord. (1 Chronicles 9:22-23)

I take younger generations with me when I minister; it is my greatest joy to do this. I am excited about what I see in them, I am excited when I see them living out the values that are dear to me, but I am always conscious that my living testimony among them will be the clearest message they receive. As we travel together I enjoy it, they enjoy it and I believe this is the way God wants us to pass on what he has so graciously given us.

One of the most humbling experiences of my life was when a 20-year-old girl from South Africa came to catch the heartbeat of what God was doing. She shared my life for six weeks. When she went home she said to me, 'I have lived with you for six weeks and nothing you have said or done has contradicted the message you give.'

I am custodian of a vision. I do not have 'a ministry'. I have a vision. If I do not pass on that vision then I have not been a good steward. The next generation will take it further, they will allow God to refine it. It will blossom and grow, and they will pass it on to the next generation. One day I will see it in all its glory. That privilege will not be mine if I do not pass it on.

We need to expect and rejoice in the day when we see a generation pushing us out of office.

They will rise up as we include them, as we pass on to them and as they see us living in the anointing the way God intended us to: honouring them and loving them as we go along the way. Just as Jesus did with his disciples.

They can do it!

'Before I formed you in the womb I knew you, before you were born I set you apart; I appointed you as a prophet to the nations.' 'Ah, sovereign Lord,' I said, 'I do not know how to speak; I am only a youth.' But the Lord said to me, 'Do not say "I am only a youth." You must go to everyone I send you to and say whatever I command you. Do not be afraid of them, for I am with you and will rescue you.' Then the Lord reached out his hand and touched my mouth and said to me, 'Now, I have put my words in your mouth. See, today I appoint you over nations and kingdoms to uproot and tear down, to destroy and overthrow, to build and to plant.' (Jeremiah 1:5-10)

Jeremiah was appointed in the womb, chosen as a prophet to the nations. There are children and young people who have been chosen and appointed by the Almighty God for the nations, even before they were born. They may feel inferior because of their youth, just as Jeremiah did. Today he is calling us to be his mouthpiece to them, telling them to not be afraid, telling them that we will be there for them, encouraging and supporting them every step of the way.

God has trusted them with his words; he has appointed them to speak to nations and kingdoms. So often we feel unsupported; there seems to be no one to come alongside us yet there is a generation wanting to be released. They are our co-workers, our disciples. The anointing entrusted to us is theirs too. God gives us our Elishas and Jeremiahs! Let no one despise youth. Be their champions!

The generations together

Psalm 133 says, 'How good and pleasant it is when brothers dwell together in unity.' The word 'brothers' is from Greek (*adelphoi*) which means 'coming from the same womb', so it could be said to be a generational expression! God takes such delight in unity that he commands blessing into it. It is sad that so many people think that having the other generations around prevents unity, rather than being an expression of it.

Jesus said, 'By this shall all men know that you are my disciples, when you have love one for another.' (John 13:35)

That includes the witness of generations committed to each other and being bound together with cords of love that cannot be broken. Can you imagine the Body of Christ flowing together like that? This vision is found in the Word of God!

The first step to seeing that unity is to discover where children and young people are found in the Bible. Most people could recall specific verses where they are mentioned, e.g. Samuel, Matthew 18, Jairus' daughter, Josiah. However they are actually interwoven throughout the Bible. They are missed because they are hidden in words like 'people', 'all', 'everyone', 'whosoever', 'the entire nation', 'the entire community', and 'household'. The majority of the time we can safely presume that these words included children, young people, the elderly, men, women, babies.

We miss this because we have made the word 'everyone' mean adults. Let me give you an example. In most churches, if the minister said, 'I want everybody at a prayer meeting tonight at 8 o'clock,' how many would go home and get the babies? How many would make sure the children had an afternoon sleep so they could attend? How many teenagers would automatically come?

'Everyone' means from the youngest to the oldest. If the Bible was reread with this simple revelation the picture of the generations living and moving together would be unfolded in a dramatic way.

Let's look at a few examples of this:

Together to be accountable

In Exodus 16 we read,

> Then Moses told Aaron, 'Say to the entire Israelite community, come before the Lord, for he has heard your grumbling.'

Here is an example where the children, young people, were called with the adults to stand before God. Now you might ask why the children were there. Children hear when there is grumbling and complaining so they were already a part of it by the actions of the adults. There were probably many reasons why God called them to account, but one of them could be that if the adults were doing this in front of them, they needed to see that God was not pleased. Also, they were probably involved too because grumbling and complaining is infectious and adult attitudes are easily caught by children.

So, the entire Israelite community was accountable to God, and that included the children and the young people within the context of their families.

How many times do we hold every generation accountable to God in an appropriate way?

Together in vision

In Exodus 17:

> The whole Israelite community set out from the Desert of Sin, travelling from place to place as the Lord had commanded.

Moses had been to Pharaoh with a message from God: 'Let my people go.' At one time Pharaoh said, 'The Lord had better be with you when I let you and your little ones go! Beware evil is ahead of you.'

He tried to use a fear of the dangers of the future to hold back the purposes of God, mentioning the children as an additional 'threat'. The plans of the enemy are often colluded with by our fear for 'our little ones'. God has plans for 'everyone', plans that involve us moving together into the vision he has for us. He has plans to take us all out of Egypt and into the Promised Land. If this involves battles along the way then he intends that we take the land together.

Sadly I see in many places that the church has three visions, one for the adults, one for the children and one for the young people. So often the vision statement of the church is not even known by the children and young people. God asks us to go together, we need each other on the journey!

Eventually the Israelites called the miracle of their liberation a curse. They lost the vision when the problems came; the children were the excuse they used to complain to God.

How often do we hear God's people saying, 'We brought our children into this and now look at the problems we are facing. This won't be any good for them.'

Don't put the children and young people on one side. Take them with you. Tell them that every generation can journey together and that they have their place on that journey! Have one vision! Imagine the forces of hell trembling as the whole army of God moves together.

Together through the problems

Some men came and told Jehoshaphat, 'A great multitude is coming against you from beyond the sea, from Syria,' and Jehoshaphat feared and set himself to seek the Lord and proclaimed a fast through all Judah. (2 Chronicles 20:2-3)

Verses 13-15: Now all Judah, with their little ones, their wives and their children, stood before the Lord. Then the Spirit of the Lord came upon Jahaziel, the son of Zechariah. And he said, 'Listen, all you of Judah and all you inhabitants of Jerusalem and you, King Jehoshaphat, thus says the Lord to you, "Do not be afraid or dismayed because of this great multitude, for the battle is not yours but God's."'

Verse 18: And Jehoshaphat bowed his head with his face to the ground and all Judah and the inhabitants of Jerusalem bowed before the Lord.

Verse 27: And they returned, every man of Judah and Jerusalem, with Jehoshaphat in front of them to go back to Jerusalem with joy, for the Lord had made them rejoice over their enemies.

Here the vast multitude are coming down against the people of Judah so Jehoshaphat calls 'the men, the women, the children, the babes in arms', to fast and pray.

When we have a problem within the Church or within the home, do we require each generation to take their place in fasting and prayer, are they all told appropriately about the problems?

It is sometimes said that children should be protected from problems. But generally, it is not the problems that cause problems to the children and young people; it is how we deal with the problems that cause them problems! Of course there are some things they need to be protected from, and how we tell them is important but generally they already know. The problem is that we don't want to recognise that they know! I have talked to too many young people and children whose parents would be appalled if they were aware of what their children had seen and heard.

We need to be an example of how to conquer and walk through problems!

Those children in Jehoshaphat's time would have known the armies were coming; they would have heard the adults talking and sensed the fear. Jehoshaphat included them, and recognised the necessity of everyone, including the babies coming before the Lord. Everybody really meant everybody!

With the armies advancing they saw the Spirit of the Lord poured out; they were part of the victory, and bowed down and worshipped God. They experienced what their God had done with their parents, and as part of their community.

Perhaps our fear of including the children and young people comes through our lack of faith for the victory. Perhaps from our underestimating what God can do through them, or our pride that we can do it without them, or lack of understanding about our interdependence. I believe it is because we have lost the vision and the lifestyle! To the people of Judah it was a way of life, a part of their heritage.

Those children would have known what to do when they had a problem at school the next day. If they stood before the Lord, he could deal with their problems.

God forgive us that we think that we can be most effective without including the children and young people. Can the hand say to the foot, 'I don't need you'? (1 Corinthians 12).

The time is coming when we will no longer want to come before the throne without the children and young people being with us. He is rekindling that desire in his people. In fact, I believe the time is coming when we won't be able to keep the children away. They are going to storm our gates and demand their place! Let's invite them before they storm!

Together to hear the Word (in the assembly)

Assemble the people – men women and children, and the aliens living in your towns – so they can listen and learn to fear the Lord your God and follow carefully all the words of this law. Their children, who do not know this law, must hear it and learn to fear the Lord your God as long as you live in the land you are crossing the Jordan to possess. (Deuteronomy 31:12-13)

Joshua read all the words of the law – the blessings and the curses – just as it is written in the Book of the Law. There was not a word of all that Moses had commanded that Joshua did not read to the whole assembly of Israel, including the women and the children, and the aliens who lived among them. (Joshua 8:34-35)

I had considered just repeating that verse several times without any comment! The children listened to pages and pages being read, sometimes I feel we have so little faith for what we can do together!

These children and young people did not have computer games to keep them happy, or pens and paper to write on. They had the anointing and respect for Joshua, they had parents who expected them to be there, and some of them had never heard the law before. It was read and they listened. This was the lifestyle and expectation.

God forgive us that we think our children can't sit through one sermon. Those children sat through the law. The Jews, the Muslims, the Jehovah's Witnesses, all have their children involved. It is time to bring our children back.

Let's cry out to God for the restoration of this blessing. To birth in the heart of every generation a desire for the Word of God that surpasses ages and generations. A desire that is focused on what God has to say to us. It will happen not through our structures but through our faith and vision.

Children in my own church had been listening to a visiting preacher for three hours. I asked them, 'How did that go?' They replied, 'It was a long time, but it was wonderful.' That's probably what the adults felt as well!

We must start to have more faith for our children. Faith for them to have more, go further and to do more; for us to be able to hear the Word of the Lord together just as God commanded Moses and Joshua.

Together in worship and celebration

> There in the presence of the Lord your God, you and your families shall eat and rejoice in everything you have put your hand to, because the Lord your God has blessed you. (Deuteronomy 12:7)

The generations together in the presence of the Lord. How can the presence of the Lord be only for one generation?

> Verse 11: Then to the place the Lord your God will choose as a dwelling for his name . . .

> Verse 12: And there rejoice before the Lord your God, you, your sons and daughters, your menservants and maid-servants . . .

The place that God had chosen as a dwelling for his Name – a place for every generation to rejoice. They were commanded to rejoice before the Lord. When they rejoiced they knew whom they were rejoicing about, they knew that they were coming into their heritage. They knew what God had done.

> And on that day they offered great sacrifices, rejoicing because God had given them great joy. The women and children also rejoiced. The sound of rejoicing in Jerusalem could be heard far away. (Nehemiah 12:43)

This was the dedication of the wall of Jerusalem when God gave them great joy. Joy was the gift from God. All of them were recipients, all expected to receive, all were available to receive and all manifested that joy. 'When the wall was built,' it says, 'the sound of rejoicing was heard afar off.' Could this be because the children were there too?

Together in fasting

> Has anything ever happened like this in your days or in the days of your forefathers? Tell it to your children, and let your children tell it to their children, and their children to the next generation. What the locust swarm has left, the great locusts have eaten. (Joel 1:2-4a)

> Declare a sacred fast. Gather the people, consecrate the assembly; bring together the elders, gather the children, those nursing at the breast. Let the bridegroom leave his room and the bride her chamber. Let the priests, who minister before the Lord, weep between the temple porch and the altar. Let them say, 'Spare your people, O Lord.' (Joel 2:16)

> Verse 18: THEN the Lord will be jealous for his land and take pity on his people ... Verse 25: I will repay you for the years the locusts have eaten.

The first command was to make their children totally aware of what had happened, and to instil it in them to pass this on generationally. The children understood the severity of the situation, they came with understanding, they came with the same heart cry, 'Spare your people [every generation], O Lord.'

'THEN the Lord will take pity, THEN the Lord will restore.' A commanded blessing instead of the curse, a spirit of unity to advance. A whole nation in unity, every generation fasting and praying. Every generation with one heart-cry.

Can we raise again one cry from the whole community of God, a heart-cry for holiness, a heart-cry for our nation, a heart-cry for the world? 'Spare your people, O Lord'!

The generations were together in many different circumstances. We need restoration to bring every generation including the children, to where the action is, to where the presence of God is. Bring the children into the anointing. Sometimes we feel we have to protect God from the children. The anointing doesn't run away because children come in, the anointing is for everyone.

Each occasion we have mentioned is centred on the presence and the workings of God. Coming together is not about us; it is about the presence of God!

He will do whatever needs to be done when we release him to change our hearts and renew our minds. This is not about implementing structures to bring us together; it is about bringing repentance, holiness and a passion for the presence of Jesus. He who called the generations from the beginning will release each one into their destiny and each one to flow in absolute harmony with the others. This is the divine orchestration of God.

Taking the nations

God said to Joshua, 'Go over this Jordan, you and all this people [men, women, young people and children], into the land which I am giving to them [every generation], the Israelites. Every place upon which the sole of your foot shall tread, that I have given to you, as I promised Moses.' (Joshua 1:2-3)

This is still the command of God. There is land that is ours; there are communities, cities, nations that belong to the most high God. He has given the nations (every man, woman and child) to Jesus as his heritage.

The land was promised as every generation advanced. This verse is often quoted without any mention of the children and young people being involved. Together they entered the land and took the territory God had promised them.

There is a rallying cry for every generation to take their place. The vision is one vision, the call is one call. We can support and enable each other to take the land. We can win the world together, and fulfil the great commission.

All the ends of the earth will remember and turn to the Lord, and all the families of the nations will bow down before him, for dominion belongs to the Lord and he rules over the nations. . . . Future generations will be told about the Lord. They will proclaim his righteousness to a people yet unborn – for he has done it.' (Psalm 22:27, 30, 31)

Here is the promise, 'all the families of the nations' – men, women and children bowing down before him. We are in the day that David never lived to see.

I will perpetuate your memory through all generations, therefore the nations will praise you. (Psalm 45:17)

We must never forget that the very reason that the church exists is to perpetuate the name of Jesus and to ensure that those he died for get to hear about it. This is why we must move outside our own physical generations, why we must raise up spiritual children, why we must go to the ends of the earth.

God calls families: I am called and so are my children. We go together into the nations and they will nurture their children to see the nations turn to Jesus. Many would think this call was too demanding, or too radical for their children, but Genesis 22:17 says, 'Because you have not withheld your son . . . your descendants will take the gates of the city.' Don't withhold your children from the great commission because in this sacrifice is the blessing for the generations to come.

Raising a generation with a passion for the world

There is no excuse for delaying the equipping of every saint for the work of the ministry. 'Every saint' includes the children and young people. This is the time to equip them to go, to give them a vision for the world, to raise them as a generation who are sent, who will take the nations.

Previous generations have raised a few with a passion for the lost; today's vision is that this generation lives a passion for the lost.

Children and young people are ready for revival, they are ready to be militant, and they are ready for the power of God that was given so that the harvest could be gathered in.

Among our children and young people are labourers we have prayed for, don't let them pass you by. Put the world in their hearts, and the weapons in their hands, protect them as they go and see the nations change; your nation, every nation.

Prayer

Lord we come, mindful of a wounded and broken society, but even more of the broken and wounded Body of Christ. In this nation, and across the world we see the brokenness of your Body, which causes you such pain. A Body that is fractured and broken, a Body where you said that we should love one another. We come now in repentance, for we have been part of something that has caused your heart such pain.

We come before you, offering ourselves. We may not know where you will take us or what you might call us to do but we come and say to you, Lord, we will stand in the gap. Please would you use us to repair the breach. We don't know what it's going to cost, but, we are prepared to do this because we love our nation, we love your body, we love this land, and above all we love you.

So we ask you to hold back the curse on our nation. We know you are looking for people who would stand in the gap, and we are offering ourselves, knowing that when you look for people, you equip them, empower them, and send the Holy Spirit on them, giving them everything necessary for the task.

As the fractures are healed we wait for the blessing, even to a thousand generations. We receive our heritage and commit to pass on all that you have entrusted to us.

And so, Lord God, would you bless and use us and our families, to release a healing through the generations, raising up fathers, releasing the young people, freeing the children that we might be one in our city, in this nation, and for all the nations. Amen.